The Pocket
Mentor

The Pocket Mentor

Essential Advice for
Aspiring Executives

Harry Hoffman

**Andrews McMeel
Publishing**

Kansas City

www.andrewsmcmeel.com

98 99 00 01 02 QUF 10 9 8 7 6 5 4 3 2 1

Library of Congress Cataloging-in-Publication Data:

Hoffman, Harry.
    The pocket mentor : essential advice for aspiring
executives / Harry Hoffman.
        p.   cm.
    ISBN 0-8362-6764-8
    1. Industrial management. 2. Success in business.
HD31.H5598   1998
650.1—dc21   98-7096
                                        CIP

For

Jan, Harry, and Lori

Contents

Developing Your Management Style

Practical Matters

On Leadership

Foreword

I met Harry Hoffman in December 1976 when I began working at Ingram Book Company. In September of 1977, as vice president of finance, I began reporting directly to Harry. Working with Harry was one of the highlights of my professional career and our close personal friendship continues to this day. He was a very valuable and important mentor to me and he still is.

Harry has incredible people skills. You always knew he was in charge, but he was very warm with the people who wanted to make a contribution and very open to their ideas. You really felt good about the time you spent with him: you were part of a team, you were being heard, and your efforts were appreciated. Ingram Book was growing rapidly, but it wasn't a big company in the late seventies. The people who reported to Harry became a close-knit group, going out to lunch together every day. We were having such a good time with the business, and Harry was the driver of that.

Harry didn't get into a lot of detail, but he had an amazing ability to skim through a great deal of information, get to the top of it, and then focus on key issues. At our daily meeting, he always offered or turned up what we began to call the "idea of the day." He would say, "Here's an idea, how can we approach it, does it make any sense?" The tremendous success of Ingram was in large part due to those ideas. Maybe only 10 percent of them were ever implemented, but because of the creative environment, there were so many ideas we could pursue.

At Ingram, and later at Waldenbooks, Harry pushed through a lot of things that were absolutely industry changing, both in wholesale distribution and in retailing. The genius of developing a demand wholesaler for books was basically Harry's genius—the idea of having a broad selection of titles from many publishers which could be ordered easily and shipped rapidly, in one shipment to a bookstore. He came up with the idea of using microfiche as a way of putting a constantly changing catalog together, established computer online order entry at Ingram when it was still a new concept, and later established a chain retail distribution center when he was at Waldenbooks.

In my opinion, Harry has done more to get "books to readers" than probably anyone else in the twentieth century with the possible exception of Oprah Winfrey.

But it wasn't always his constant barrage of ideas or his plans that we listened to at Ingram. He had a wonderful ability to stimulate thought, and there was an openness and acceptance in all communication. You never had to worry that you would get shot down for a silly idea or a silly way to implement an idea. Often the silly or "impossible" ideas worked when they were implemented, and major breakthroughs in how we did business were achieved. It was a very creative environment.

Philip M. Pfeffer
President and Chief Operating Officer
Random House, Inc.

Preface

Fighting a Culture of Fear

The CEOs of today are afraid. They are afraid of the specter of Wall Street looking over their shoulders and demanding positive results on a monthly or quarterly schedule. They are afraid they might not be in compliance with the many rules and regulations of our society. They are afraid there may be someone waiting in the wings who can perform their jobs better than they can.

The fear that motivates a company's managers is passed down to its employees through outrageous demands that can hinder the future growth and health of the company. Innovation, creativity, and invention are stifled when creative people are sacrificed to a mentality that overemphasizes numbers and regulations and short-term thinking. For young people just out of college, this fear can be a serious impediment to the development of a successful career.

In this book I offer you a set of basic management principles that can assist you as you begin your career, or that can help you revive a career that has stagnated. By the time you finish reading this book you will have learned how to make choices that will counteract the destructive nature of a culture of fear. I have included accounts of some of my own experiences in the corporate world so that you may acquire insights from real-life challenges as well as from the more general principles in the rest of the book.

To get the most out of this book, carry it with you. Refer to it often. Reread sections at different stages of your career. As you gain experience, you will see many things in a new light, and you will continue to expand your knowledge and understanding as you develop a successful management style.

Acknowledgments

With love and gratitude, I would like to acknowledge the wonderful gift that Jan Keeling, my daughter, gave to me when she concluded that my reflections had merit and agreed to be my agent and editor.

Thanks to Ashley Crownover for your invaluable editorial assistance, to Randy O'Brien for your interviewing skills, and to Matt Lombardi at Andrews McMeel for your capacity to help me make clear what I wanted to say.

I will always be grateful to the late Bronson Ingram, who got me started in this business I love. I am grateful to George Hopkins and Tom Thornton for believing that after all my years of distributing and selling books, I could actually write one.

To my island friends, Kim and Kelly Templeton, thanks for your affection and support. Special recognition to Norma Hoffman, who shared the path of my corporate journey. My appreciation also goes to Phil Pfeffer. I was proud to consider myself his mentor, but I also knew just how much I was learning from him.

Introduction

I suspect that my high school teachers and college professors did not think I had much of a chance of being successful in life. Getting through high school was not too traumatic, but getting through college was another story. Someone told me I was a prime example of the "gentleman C scholar." I wasn't wild, nor was I irresponsible. I just found school boring, and I disliked studying. I lacked direction and purpose. I didn't have a cause and was intimidated by those who did.

After college I did the things that were expected of me. I got a job, I got married, and I had three children. I was adventurous enough to seek and gain employment as an FBI agent, but to this day I am not sure what motivated me, except that I had to work to support my growing family. After three rather nondescript years in the Bureau, I decided that the pay was not enough to support a family, so I left the Bureau and entered the business world.

Over the next thirteen years I had modest success in sales and marketing with Procter and Gamble, Bell and Howell, and a small company in Madison, Wisconsin, called Demco Library Supplies. At the age of thirty-five, while I was still working for Bell and Howell, I came to the realization that I knew more about the business of selling and marketing cameras and projectors than my bosses did. It had taken me too many years to realize that just because a person occupies a position of power in a company, that person is not necessarily the best one for the position. I had always been intimidated by bosses and their power. Now, at thirty-five, I began to think that I might be as smart as (or smarter than) the people who directed me. I decided to change my approach.

I went from being a somewhat passive person to being someone who could take on the responsibility of rocking the boat and making the changes that I thought would improve the company. I became much more assertive and told literally everyone in the company how I felt about the way things were going. My bosses implemented some of my ideas and liked the results. This earned me several promotions in rapid order, and for the first time in my life I had the confidence necessary to take the actions I felt would improve the way the companies I worked for did business.

I set about trying to change what I didn't agree with. As I gained more power through promotions, this became easier to do. During this "realization period," I set a goal for myself to become the CEO of some company (any company) by the time I was forty. Setting this rather simple but ambitious goal was significant. It meant that my actions during that stage of my career would be directed toward reaching that goal.

It actually took me seven years to become a CEO (at age forty-two), but I'm convinced that I would never have made it if I had not reached the "realization period" of my life and if I had not set that goal. I sometimes regret that it didn't happen faster, and I believe it could have if I had had a mentor.

And that is why I wrote this book. The precepts in this book are those I learned on my own (from failures as well as successes) and which helped me in my career. They are relatively simple and straightforward. If followed, they will be of help to anyone who sets a goal to become a key executive of a company—maybe even before the age of forty-two.

Starting
Out

Who Are You?

The answer to this question will help you build a satisfying career.

I t may be difficult for you to answer this question. You may be too influenced by society, your parents, and your friends to be able to take a truly objective view of who you are and what you would like to do with your life. But you should recognize that work will take up a significant part of your waking hours for the next forty or fifty years. If you allow outside pressures to force you into pursuing a field or occupation that you don't really like, you will have a great deal of difficulty becoming successful. You will probably be unhappy as well, one of the many who lead "lives of quiet desperation."

Without having acquired any knowledge of the "real world," graduates may take any job that comes along, hoping that the business they choose is one in which they will thrive. In most cases, such a person will *not* thrive. He or she is probably poorly prepared to deal with the politics and personalities of the new company, not to mention the complexities of the job itself. This can lead to cynicism and dislike of the very thing that consumes most of the day. As more money is earned and responsibilities are added, the individual can find him- or herself trapped in a job, without much hope of finding an enjoyable occupation.

The question itself—"Who are you?"—should not be seen as a trap. You don't have to come up with a set of "correct" answers. But if you are going to lead a happy, productive life, it is important to make a pass right now at answering the question. Try to answer it honestly, looking at how you feel about yourself and the things you think you're good at. Remember to ignore the pressures of society and family, and understand that who you really are is the person with whom you must live the rest of your life . . . preferably in harmony.

The Self-Evaluation

Define your interests, strengths, and weaknesses.

Take time to sit down and think and write about yourself and your career: your strengths, your weaknesses, and the things you feel you can do to become stronger.

This can start with an assessment of how you feel about people in general. There are very few declared misanthropes, but unless you really enjoy interaction with others you should consider a career that does not require you to be on stage at all times. A job that allows you to work by yourself may be the answer.

I have noticed that people who are good in sales really like convincing others that they should buy a product. Do you get a thrill out of influencing people? Perhaps you can find a product you really believe in and find a job selling that product.

A person who loves numbers may find it difficult to become a "people person." Such a person might do quite well in a financial or accounting department.

Evaluate yourself in several areas. Here is a list of areas to help you get started. (As you acquire more experience, of course, you will learn more about your strengths and weaknesses.)

Ability to motivate people
Artistic skills
Creative talent
Financial skills
Marketing skills
Computer skills
Production skills
Other technical skills
Skill in analyzing systems
Skill in creating systems

After you begin working for a company, and throughout your career, you should periodically give yourself a self-review. Write down the things you do well (and perhaps should be rewarded for) and the things you do fairly well (but could work to improve). Then list the tasks or areas you do not do well in, and outline a plan to correct these deficiencies. You may want to take a look at your résumé or your review from the previous year to stimulate your thinking about your accomplishments, the things you have learned on the job, and your areas of growth.

Avoiding a Life of Quiet Desperation

Keep your own interests and abilities in mind.

I grew up in an age when there was little or no recognition of the fact that there are major differences in the innate capacities of individuals. In school I always struggled with science and math. I was led to believe that the reason I did poorly was that I did not apply myself or study hard enough. I did well in history, English, and other subjects that did not require scientific or technical aptitude.

It wasn't until much later in life that I accepted the fact that I wasn't lazy or a bad student. I realized that I had little or no interest in some subjects and that society was wrong to criticize my study habits or my ability to learn. Of course it is necessary to learn basic skills, but requiring students to put long, dreary, unproductive hours into the study of subjects in which they have little interest is a mistake. I strongly believe that teachers should spend more time determining the interests and aptitudes of a student and helping the student pursue those interests.

We are all different: Some of us have high IQs; some have the ability to comprehend things quickly; some have a talent for interpersonal relationships; some are more creative than others. Some of us like to work with numbers and the facts, while others prefer to create and work with abstractions.

You may be in a situation that you feel prevents you from pursuing your true interests: It may be impossible to relocate, you may be already established in a job or career, or pressures such as family responsibility may make you feel you have little choice.

It is still important to do your self-evaluation. Promise yourself that you will be on the lookout for any opportunities that might allow you to leave an unsuitable job. Your self-evaluation will give focus to your awareness. At the same time, remember that even though it is most important to capitalize on our strengths, we all have the power to improve in areas where there might be deficiencies. Becoming more of a "numbers person" is possible through proper study. The same is true of becoming a more creative thinker, or a "people person." No matter what you believe your strengths or weaknesses to be, you can always improve and become a higher achiever.

There are some things you can do every day to become better prepared for your future. Pay attention and listen. Learn how to evaluate others as well as yourself. Take advantage of any learning opportunities that arise. Talk to people who are more experienced than you are.

Understanding Corporate Culture

Learning about the culture of a company is at least as important as learning how to perform effectively the work that is assigned to you.

To understand the culture of your company, look first to the CEO. Often it is his or her personality, training, background, and prejudices that determine a company's nature. The culture may be benevolent or despotic, or it may be one that really does not have a clear sense of direction.

Corporate Culture Type 1

If a company's culture is benevolent, the CEO is usually easygoing and friendly, a person who prides him- or herself on developing a feeling of caring within the company. The CEO will manage "by walking around," and will probably manage "by expectation." Some believe this is the best possible culture, but it can be demanding at times. The expectations of the CEO may not be completely defined. Employees may go slightly crazy trying to live up to what they think these expectations might be.

While this is often an undisciplined culture, it is usually highly creative. The CEO may have more respect for ideas and innovation than for numbers.

Because of the short-term thinking that exists in American business today, placing more value on ideas and innovation than on numbers may lead to difficulties with Wall Street, bankers, and shareholders. But if you thrive on ideas and innovation and want to work for a company that gives high priority to developing new products and programs, this may be the best kind of working environment for you.

You will see a bias toward this type of culture throughout the book. It is my personal favorite type of business culture, which is probably why I call it Type 1!

Corporate Culture Type 2

A despotic or tyrannical culture sounds terrible, but there are many who actually enjoy working for a company of this nature. In this type of environment, the CEO rigidly sets the course for the company and will probably manage "by objectives." The CEO is a tough boss and takes pride in being considered tough.

The CEO in this type of company may perform brilliantly, but will probably create an environment where mistakes are not long tolerated. Because of this, very few in the company will want to take risks and creativity may not be valued. Turnover may be high, but those who leave will feel that they have received excellent training. If you take direction well and like to know exactly what your responsibilities are, this culture might be right for you.

Corporate Culture Type 3

A third type of company is one in which the CEO does not really know what is going on in the company or in the marketplace. In this kind of culture, the CEO may be inexperienced or lacking in leadership talent, and so may have delegated the power of his or her office to two or three vice presidents. These vice presidents will do just about anything to maintain the status quo because they are the ones who really hold the power.

This is usually not a very happy culture. There may be a lot of antagonism between the vice presidents and the other managers in the company, who would prefer that the real boss be the boss. These other managers may not like the driving force to come from two or three other people, who will often use their power to keep others down. If the CEO is the driving force, he or she is more likely to have a balanced view of (and give balanced treatment to) everyone in the company.

Before You Take a Job

Know who and what you'll be
working for.

Before you accept a job, try to find out as much as you can about the company. Talk to the people who work there. Ask them questions about the CEO. Is he or she autocratic? Is he or she benevolent? Most important, is he or she open and accessible to people in the company?

If you are being seriously considered for a management or executive training position, before any decisions are made you will probably meet with a lot of people who work for the company. You can take these opportunities to use subtle questioning to find out if this is the kind of company you would like to work for. If you meet with someone who seems willing to talk about the company, strike up a rapport and ask questions. The questions you ask may be divided into four categories.

1. Ask about the financial strength of the company.

What is this company's financial strength? (You might ask if you can take a look at a balance sheet and a profit-and-loss statement.)

2. Ask about the company's competition.

Who are your strongest competitors? What are they like? (You should know a little bit about the answer to this question from your own research.)

How does this company stack up when compared to the competition?

How do the products and services stack up?

Why is the company better than its competition?

If your company is not better than the competition, why not? What is the company doing to become better than the competition?

3. Try to find out how the people who work there feel about working for the company.

Are you happy with the company?

Are you happy with management?

Are you happy with the company's products?

4. Make sure the company is not locked into the "If it ain't broke, don't fix it!" mentality.

Is this company willing to make changes for the better?

The Organization's Structure

Understanding the way a company is organized will help you perform your job more effectively.

There are many different ways a business can be structured, but basically a company is made up of the following areas:

1. Office of the president and CEO
2. The financial area
3. The sales and marketing area
4. The administrative area
5. The MIS (management information systems) area
6. The distribution area

There are, of course, other areas within companies, such as human resources, research and development, testing, catalog/direct response, and telephone sales. Ask your boss to give you an overview of the way your company is organized. If there is an organization chart, ask if you can have a copy of it. If you cannot acquire one, put together your own chart based on the information you collect by talking to people in the company.

Motivate yourself to talk with everyone in the company to find out what they do in the company and how they do it. Showing friendly interest can go a long way toward gathering the information that will help you get an overview of how the different parts of the company work together.

The Big Picture

Evaluating Your Company

Write about it.

Y ou should make an evaluation of your company from time to time, just as you do of yourself. Write down the things that are good about the company from your perspective (its strengths), the things that are bad (its weaknesses), and, most important, things you can do to capitalize on the strengths and help eliminate the weaknesses.

Here are a few simple exercises that you should do periodically:

1. Restructure (on paper) your company or your department.

Determine the best possible organization for getting things done more effectively. Is the organization structured properly to take advantage of current business opportunities? Are people who perform the various functions reporting to the appropriate department heads? Is it clear to all who reports to whom? Consider the strengths and weaknesses of those who are managing the business, and think about whether or not these managers are properly positioned. (For example, is the manager of human resources really a person who cares about people? Is the sales manager a high-energy person who knows how to motivate people? Is the operations manager an organized person who cares about creating and maintaining effective systems?)

2. Make your own evaluation of bosses, peers, and subordinates.

Include their strengths, weaknesses, and whether they seem to be properly positioned in the company. It is terribly important to be honest as you make these evaluations. Be objective and keep your personal likes and dislikes out of the evaluations.

3. Evaluate the company programs and policies with which you are familiar.

These can be personnel programs, marketing programs, or any other programs or policies that have an effect on the company's success. If you feel you could make improvements or changes in the programs, write down the things you would like to do.

4. Read about other businesses.

You may have already gained experience with other companies. What have you discovered that other companies are doing better than your company? Are they doing things your company should be doing or has the capacity to do? What can your company do better than its competitors?

5. Write down how you think your company is perceived by the customer or consumer.

What actions could be taken to improve this perception?

These exercises are helpful in several ways. Performing these exercises will broaden your knowledge of your company and improve your perspective. You will better understand why your company does things the way it does, and you may develop superior ways to accomplish the same objectives. Finally, you will be prepared to discuss your ideas if an unexpected opportunity arises.

You Are What You Read

Reading can be extremely important in building a successful career.

L earning how to read rapidly and learning how to absorb what you read is important not only to your personal growth, but to your career. You can build these skills with practice or by taking one of the many reading courses offered today.

As you progress in your career, you will find that the amount of "company" reading you are required to do increases significantly. While being able to understand and quickly absorb these documents is important, the reading you do in your free time can be equally important.

If you do not know or have some understanding of what is going on in your community and in the world, you will be left behind. If you do not read the important newspapers, books, and magazines, you will not be able to create new ideas to improve your business and you will not be able to respond effectively to those who do.

If you are not a "reader," you must become one. It has been said that the only correlation that can be made with a person's success is the size of that person's vocabulary. Reading is perhaps the best way to add to vocabulary as well as to add to one's overall knowledge.

Continuing Your Education

Continue to learn at every
stage of your career.

K eep learning new skills, and learn how to enhance
the skills you already have. If you can continue your
formal education, it will be helpful to take business
courses. If you have the time and money to earn a master's degree in business administration, you may have an
advantage over someone who is not able to do so. But
having an M.B.A. is not always essential and is probably
not the most important part of a manager's education.
Those who have M.B.A.s are undoubtedly well prepared
for many things, especially in the area of finance, but at
times they may lose their perspective on the human side
of management. An icon in retailing perhaps put it best
when he said, "M.B.A.s have it here [pointing to his
head], but somehow lose it here [pointing to his heart]."
In my experience, this statement is frankly true of many
M.B.A.s—although I believe many of the better schools
offering M.B.A. degrees have changed and are now
putting more emphasis on the human side of management. Remember to listen with your heart as well as
your head.

If you cannot get an M.B.A., there are many other

things you can do to keep learning. Evaluate your skills and determine the areas that need improvement. My financial skills were limited after I graduated from my liberal arts college, and I think even today liberal arts schools are not putting enough emphasis on financial courses. If you too are limited in that area, you will find it pays big dividends to take some extra courses in finance—not only for the sake of your business career, but for the sake of better managing your own finances.

It is equally important to assess your ability to speak in public. Whether you are holding a small meeting or attending a large annual meeting of stockholders, it is as important to be able to speak with confidence as it is to know what you are talking about. I have heard some managers scoff at the idea of taking a Dale Carnegie course, but such a course can help you gain confidence as well as learn how to speak in public.

For those times when you do have to speak, it is important to make sure you know how to use the English language properly. Using incorrect words or awkward sentence structure will put negative thoughts in the minds of your listeners as quickly as anything you do. If you need a little assistance brushing up on your language skills (and who doesn't?), there are some books that can help. One small book in particular, *The Elements of Style*, by William Strunk Jr. and E. B. White, should be in everyone's library. It is the bible of the correct use of the English language. And it always helps to rehearse your speech before a sympathetic listener, such as your spouse or a friend.

Reading books on management by Peter Drucker, Tom Peters, and other knowledgeable authors will undoubtedly offer many new learning experiences. It is also imperative that you read at least three newspapers a day. I would choose three of these four: the *Wall Street Journal*, the *New York Times, Investors Business Daily*, and *USA Today*. Obviously you will not have time to read any or all of these papers in depth, but you should go through each rapidly, reading the headlines and getting more deeply into those stories that might have an association with you or your business.

While taking courses in business and reading about business will be extremely helpful, you must do a lot of the learning on your own. The training provided by most companies is often inadequate, and you must learn through doing. If you can find a mentor in your company whom you can trust, you can frequently pass your ideas and approaches to solving problems by him or her.

Facing the Future

Where will we be?

A young person is often asked, "What do you see yourself doing in five years?" or "Where would you like to be in your career in five years?" This can be a very difficult question to answer, because someone just entering the work force is burdened with learning and getting the current job done and does not have time to think a great deal about the future. Even if the time were available, it is difficult to project where you will be in five years. You face many uncertainties in dealing with the people who will have a say in your future. You probably lack information about the plans of the company or how the company sees your role in these plans.

Yet being able to develop a view of the future is essential to building a career. You must have a view of the future in order to fill a need for a customer or to help improve the productivity of a company.

To develop this view, return to the basics. You need to know what is going on in your company, in your community, and in the world. You need to build an internal information base that can be used to help solve problems. You need to ask the questions: What are the top-priority problems of this enterprise? What are the problems my company will face as we move into the future?

Choices

Set a long-range goal.

Throughout your career you will be faced with many choices whose outcomes will eventually determine who you are and what you become. A good way to help you deal with all these decisions is to set a simple long-range goal for yourself. This goal will depend on how you feel about your talents and your abilities as well as what motivates you and makes you happy. If you enjoy family life and having roots the most, your career will be different from the one you have if your main motivation in life is to become the head of a company. If this is your goal, there may be times, especially in the case of job changes and company-requested moves, when your family will object to a career move because of the severe uprooting that will occur. This would be the time when you reexamine your long-range goals. If a promotion requires a move and you are happy with your life, you are probably best served by turning down the opportunity. If you have decided you want to be a CEO, you will jump at taking the promotion. You will realize that turning down a move can have a negative effect on future opportunities that require a move. Your family may be displeased, but you will probably rationalize the move with thoughts of how your family will ultimately benefit from it.

A crucial decision time usually occurs ten to fifteen years after you finish school. You may find yourself reappraising your long-term goals. By now you may be happy in a good job. You and your family may be settled in a nice area, and life is pretty good. A reappraisal of a long-term goal to become a CEO can result in your deciding that the goal, although possibly attainable, is not worth the effort. Your new long-term goal will be to do the best you can in your existing job and to lead the good life. This life may not provide all the power or money you thought you wanted, but in itself it will be good. This should be a conscious decision, not one that you "evolve" into as the years go by. By making a conscious decision and acknowledging the reasons for the decision, whether it be happiness in what you are doing or perhaps an honest realization that you don't have the desire or the aptitude for more responsibility, you will probably avoid the frustration that hits many people in later life. The "lives of quiet desperation" are led by men and women who believe they have never realized their dreams. Make conscious choices and your dreams will be real, not just nagging fantasies.

If you choose to go for the leadership of a company, your attitude and your life will change. You have probably done well in the early stages of your career through hard work and talent. You will need to work harder and exhibit more talent if you are to realize your goal. Getting ahead in your career will be very important to you, and you and your family will be making sacrifices, mostly in the area of time. You will be away from home a great deal more, and at times you will not be in touch with what is happening to your family. You can, of course, make amends by trying to make the times you are together special, but it won't be the same. The real question is, is it worth it?

The answer will be different for different people. You may find you agree with the Gregory Peck character in the 1956 movie *The Man in the Gray Flannel Suit* (based on Sloan Wilson's novel). He decided that "going for the top" was not worth the cost.

But from the viewpoint of this former CEO and others, it is. If you do make it, the financial rewards will help alleviate some of the pain encountered in making it—but the biggest kick will be your opportunity to make an enterprise grow and to change the world in some way, however small.

Know When to Leave

In order to advance, you may
have to move on.

Young people often start new jobs with high hopes
and great expectations. Then time passes. Their feelings about the job, the company, and the people in
the company may change so that they dread going to
work every day. Or they may continue to like their job, the
company, and the people, but come to believe that they
are at a dead end. In either case, it is important to leave the
company if they want to avoid living a life of "quiet desperation." I have been in both situations, and fortunately
was able to leave and find more satisfying jobs.

I hated the first substantial job I had. I was modestly
successful in this job, but going to work every day was a
chore. I stayed too long in that job (four long years), learning a lot but disliking the business every day. I finally left,
and it turned out to be a wise decision.

In my next job I was again modestly successful, and
this time I liked the job, the company, and the people.
But I realized I was at a dead end when I was asked to
accept a "promotion" to manage the service department,
in spite of the fact that my whole business life had been
in sales and marketing. I knew nothing about the service

30

department and was totally unqualified for the job. I concluded that I had offended someone and that the best way to get rid of me was to "promote me to Siberia." (This often happens to an employee the boss wants to get rid of, even if he or she has a good record.) I left the company.

If you find yourself in this type of situation, you are probably well aware that there is some solace in having a steady income with benefits. But if you want to progress in your career, the only option you may have is to leave the company. One thing about which there is no question, of course, is that you must find another job before you hand in your resignation. It is much easier to secure new employment when you are already employed, and there is also great comfort in having a source of income while you search.

There should be no bad feelings on your part about looking for another position while you are currently employed. In fact, if companies were really enlightened, they would encourage people who are not happy in their jobs to come forward with the truth. The company's management should then support the employee's efforts to find another job. One unexpected consequence of coming forward might be that the employee has misread the situation, that the company really does value the employee, and that management will make changes to encourage the employee to stay.

When you find a new job and the time comes to resign, it is essential that you leave on good terms. If you have had a bad experience with the company or your boss, it may be tempting to take parting shots as you leave. But no matter how bad it might have been, you must remember that your employment record with the company will follow you the rest of your business life. An angry ending with your employer may have a negative effect on recommendations in the future.

Developing Your Management Style

Just Say It

Don't lose your audience to
verbosity or overcomplication.

Say it. But try to say it simply, and under no circumstances say more than is necessary. All too often in business, the person with a valid point to make kills the point by making the presentation too complex or too wordy.

One of the most common problems in communication is not knowing when to stop talking. Often you can chalk verbosity up to nervousness, but sometimes it is an attempt on the part of the presenter to demonstrate superior intelligence. In either case, the talker may lose the audience and fail to make the point. What is worse is that the talker may establish a reputation as an overexplainer and will be tuned out during meetings.

People make things complex for a number of reasons. Sometimes they like to impress others with their knowledge, using words and phrases that very few people can understand. Sometimes people who specialize in a field such as computers or finance forget that the majority of their associates do not understand the jargon of their specialties.

Keep what you have to say short and easily understood. Using big words may prove you have an excellent vocabulary, but the real test of how smart you are is being able to put what you have to say in words that are understood and accepted by your audience.

If You Are on the Listening End of a Long, Complex Monologue

Speak up when things become too complicated to understand.

If you are faced with a speaker whose idea of a conversation is to talk on and on about a difficult or boring subject, do not hesitate to tell the speaker that you don't understand. You may fear that you should understand and that the fault is yours. It is more than likely, however, that you are on solid ground, and the speaker will have to alter what he or she is saying to become understood by you and everyone else who is part of the conversation. You can say, "I get most of what you said, but I really don't understand this part of it." Don't be accusatory (not, "That's ridiculous, I don't understand a word you're saying").

Wait until you have been with a company for a while and have established yourself before you begin to speak up about the things you don't understand. Don't question policy initially. There may be reasons for the policy of which you are not yet aware. If so, you will appear ignorant or impulsive if you question the policy as if you know much better than those who have been there for years.

Develop Good Instincts

Improve the instincts nature
has given you.

Some people have naturally good instincts, which gives them a tremendous advantage over those who don't. Even in fields that have acquired decision-making support through the use of technology and statistics, the person who can intuitively make the right decision when something unpredictable happens has an extra edge that can make all the difference.

For example, baseball managers now use computers to review the performances of teams and players, gaining information that allows them to "play the percentages." This obviously improves the odds for success. But it is the manager with superb instincts who will be the most successful (assuming the talent at hand is equal to the competition). The instinctive manager will know when to take the pitcher out of the game or may give a steal sign more frequently than the manager who does not have good instincts. Most decisions will be based on "playing the percentages," but in those rare, important circumstances when that is not enough, the manager with great instincts will make the better decision. The same is true in the ever-evolving field of business.

I will not argue with the person who claims that the instincts that make a great baseball manager are innate. In the field of business, however, I believe the instincts so helpful in making good decisions can be developed.

The first way to begin to improve your instincts is to immerse yourself in information. The more you know, the better your subconscious mind will be able to engage in creative problem solving or generate new ideas and approaches to business issues. To a great extent, you are a product of your environment. Unless that environment is grounded in what is happening today, you will be seriously impeded in your efforts to solve problems or create new ideas.

Improving your instincts is also helped a great deal by attitude. As you develop your feelings about things you observe, try using this phrase: "I can change that and make it better."

Finally, make a conscious effort to "put yourself in the other person's shoes." Ask yourself:

1. What does this person need?
2. How can I fill this need?
3. If I were the other person, how would I respond
   - to what I say?
   - to how I say it?
   - to how I look when I say it?

Going against the Tide

You will often find that when a new idea or project is presented to a group, the majority will find fault with the idea.

R esistance to change is a way of life in most corporations, no matter how aggressive the corporation is thought to be. Very often a good idea is quashed by an outpouring of resistance from a majority of the people who may have to be involved with its implementation.

There are many reasons for this, including fear of additional work, fear that the creator of the idea may be successful and become a candidate for sought-after promotions, and—probably the dominant reason—fear of change. In my business life I have been lucky enough to create a few ideas that have had a major positive impact on the business I've been a part of. Without exception, when I presented each idea to an interested group, the group came out overwhelmingly against it. If I had listened to the group and retreated, many of the things I was able to change in the companies I worked for would never have happened, and my career and perhaps the companies themselves would not have grown as they did.

When I was at Waldenbooks I presented a program that I thought would enhance the leadership position of

my company, increase sales dramatically, and offer a plat-
form for future businesses. The idea came to me when
our sales were suffering as the country was in a recession.
(The thought process I used in generating this idea can be
found on page 76.) The idea I presented to a group of vice
presidents within the company was to provide a "frequent buyer" program aimed at creating more loyalty
among customers by offering a discount and other benefits if they joined the program. The airlines had successfully used a "frequent flyer" program, and I believed
that such a program could be used successfully in the
book industry.

When I presented the idea, I was surprised by the
amount of opposition it received. Twelve out of thirteen
people in the room were vehemently opposed and
expressed vociferous concern about the cost of the program, the possible failure of the program, and the
amount of additional work that would be necessary to
bring the program into existence. Although being the
boss made it easier for me to get my way, I made sure I
was well prepared to overcome objections such as these.

When I first began developing the idea for the program, I too believed that it would require a massive commitment of computer and programming time. To get a
better perception of what was involved, I spent a considerable amount of time with programmers and project
leaders (some of the people who would have to do the
work) to determine the idea's viability. These people were
pleased to have been brought in early on the idea. After
reviewing the program requirements, they were able to
tell me that it would be easy to do. I also spent considerable time writing out "what if" scenarios, putting down

various expectations of results, and listing pros and cons. I then consulted with people in the advertising department to help me develop graphics for an effective presentation of the program.

After all this preparation, I was able to persuade the vice presidents that the possible positive returns from the program were far greater than the extra costs. I eventually secured their enthusiastic support.

Four million subscribers signed up for this program during its first year, and overall business increased significantly. The program increased customer loyalty and also became an avenue to reach consumers by direct mail.

Become Socratic

Ask questions that promote thought and solutions to problems rather than anger and defensiveness.

People love to answer questions, especially if the questions are about themselves or their areas of expertise. But questions can irritate if the asking is done in a threatening way. It is important to develop a style of asking questions that makes people feel good. Asking people about their families, about what they have done with their lives, and about their opinions on issues that are related to the company will create a positive response.

Questioning in the proper way (a way that does not threaten) is also a great technique for getting people to think more deeply about an issue or even to change their thinking on a topic. This is what I mean by "becoming Socratic." Socrates, of course, is famous for his systematic method of questioning a person in order to draw forth an expression of truth. If someone presents you with a program that you think is flawed, your questioning technique will allow you to expose the flaws or, conversely, to give the presenter an opportunity to justify the program. It's a good idea to start with fairly easy questions that you think the person is likely to know something about.

People like to answer questions that require knowledge in their area of expertise. Later questions may be gently phrased to require more thinking from the person being questioned. This is one of the excellent qualities of the Socratic method: It allows those being questioned the opportunity to think for themselves.

If you use the Socratic questioning technique properly, you will be perceived as a thinker and a sage. If you use it improperly (in an accusatory tone or in order to tear someone down), you will be perceived as a troublemaker, one who relishes muddying the waters and damaging proposals. This is especially true if you are the boss.

Here's an example of how the "Socratic method" might be used in a business setting:

You are in a meeting in which the advertising manager has just presented a Christmas promotional program that you believe is complicated, costly, and will not get the job done. You may begin your Socratic questioning by asking permission to ask a few questions, saying something like "The program is interesting, but may I ask a few questions?" Starting this way keeps the ball in the court of the presenter—and this is where you want it to be. You want to make the presenter believe that you are simply giving him or her ample opportunity to explain how well thought out the program is.

The questions that follow should be directed toward the presenter's conception of the various elements of the program:

"How do you see the program being presented to the customer?"
"Do you think complexity is an issue?"

"Do you think we can make it an easy program to
   sell?"
"What kind of response do you expect?"

After you have finished your questioning, several
things could happen. The first is that the flaws you sus-
pected really do not exist and the program is good. In
this case, your questions have helped the presenter to
make his or her program understood. The second thing
your questioning might do is bring out obvious flaws in
the plan, indicating that the program must be changed.
This can give you an opportunity to present your own
well-thought-out program, which you have already pre-
tested with the same questions you asked of the presenter. The best way to present your alternative plan is to
begin by asking a subjective question such as "What if
. . . ?" or "What do you think of . . . ?" This technique
not only is a gentle way to turn the thinking to your proposal, but also enables everyone, including the original
presenter, to become part of the proposal.

Always Protect the People You Manage

Make your employees' well-being your first priority.

Protecting the people you manage does not mean that you should protect incompetence. Even the best organization has employees who do not measure up and who must be dealt with accordingly. Protecting your people means that you take responsibility for what they do. This responsibility includes the work they do as well as their health and welfare while performing that work.

If a person has not freely chosen a dangerous occupation, that person should not be expected to face danger for the sake of profits or ideas or for any other reason. As a boss, you may encourage your people to take risks: to risk going against the tide for the sake of an innovation that may improve the company, or to risk the disapproval of colleagues for the sake of an action that is going to benefit the company as a whole. But asking employees to risk life or limb for something they may not be willing to be sacrificed for should be against the "boss's code of honor."

Unless your people are members of the police, soldiers, rescue personnel, or others who are trained to encounter physical danger and who have made a conscious choice to enter a risky occupation, you do not have the right to expose your people to danger. An extreme example of how far the principle of protecting people can extend was the problem we at Waldenbooks faced when Salman Rushdie was condemned to death by the Ayatollah of Iran in 1989.

In 1989, Ayatollah Ruhollah Khomeini offered a multimillion-dollar bounty for the death of Salman Rushdie, author of *The Satanic Verses,* a book that offended some Islamic leaders. Bookstores were threatened with firebombings for carrying this book.

When we at Waldenbooks first heard that our stores were receiving bomb threats, our immediate thought was to protect our people. We advised our stores to pull the book off the shelves until we could learn more about what was happening. The *New York Times* learned of our action, and we were vehemently criticized by the media and the publishing community for not protecting the First Amendment.

We held our position for approximately two days, then polled our store managers to determine how they felt about the issue and their own safety. Almost all the managers said they wanted to sell the book and were not afraid. We gave them the choice of putting the book back on the shelves or, if they had deep concerns, of keeping the book in the back room to be sold only on request from customers.

As it turned out, every store in the thousand-store chain chose to put the book back on the shelves.

We received over a hundred bomb threats, and one store was set on fire (no one was injured). To this day we think we did the right thing by protecting our people first and then letting them decide if they were willing to take a risk.

Handling Difficult Situations

There are different ways
to confront someone.

When there is controversy with another, often the best solution to the problem is to face the issue squarely and address it with the individual. Arrange a meeting with your antagonist, and in an agreeable manner let the person know that you are aware of the problem, that you would like to solve the problem, and that you would like his or her help in doing so. The problem may be a personality clash or a divergent opinion on how to handle a particular project. Confronting the problem in a meeting with the person is one way to relax tensions and get something done. This is especially true when you are dealing with a peer.

If you are dealing with a boss, handling the problem on a confrontational basis becomes more difficult. A good method for handling this kind of situation is to write down the problem as you see it, along with your thoughts about a solution.

There are several advantages to presenting a written analysis of the problem to your boss. The first is that you won't torpedo your superior with a one-on-one confrontation. You will provide this person with the opportunity to think through more clearly what you have written, giving him or her a chance to see the wisdom of your position. A one-on-one confrontation can put a boss on the defensive, especially if there is a personality issue involved. A written presentation takes away the confrontational aspect along with the irrational emotional response. A letter will put a boss on the defensive as well, but in a different way: he or she must now answer you.

Figure out what you want to say and get it down on paper without concern for its appearance. Then go over it again, judging your letter by what you know about the person who will receive it. Does the person prefer communications that are terse and to the point? (You can condense your letter.) Is the person impressed by inspiring language and ideas that tie into the vision of the company? (Make sure you include some sentences that tie your idea to the company's goals.) Is the person especially fond of ideas that will save money? (Include information that shows how your idea will cut costs.) Take out any offensive remarks that you did not censor in the first stage of writing down your thoughts. Before sending off your letter or memo, read it one more time to make sure it says what you want it to say.

A lot of offices now use interoffice E-mail for communications. Using E-mail can serve the same purposes as a letter (avoiding confrontation, allowing the other person time to think before responding). Remember that E-mail's ease of use can make it tempting to send off spontaneous thoughts. I suggest you save a message in a file for a while, then look at it again before firing off what could be an embarrassingly ungrammatical or provocative message.

The Worst Advice You Can Give

"If it ain't broke, don't fix it!"

This has been a popular bit of advice given by managers for generations. But it is absolutely the worst advice anyone can give. The mark of a good manager is a constant challenging of rules, policies, and programs, along with a continual examination of products and services to see how they can be improved.

Literally everything, whether it is a product or a service, is "broke" or on its way to being "broke" from the moment it is developed and put in the marketplace. Even if a product or service is protected by patent or copyright, the chances are good that someone else is working hard to develop a variation that is even better.

You must work hard to improve new ideas, and equally hard to improve on the product or service you already have. This search for constant improvement will ensure that your company remains a powerful force in the marketplace.

Trust All . . .
but None Too Much

Have an open mind, but
keep your eyes open, too.

Most think this phrase was spoken by a famous political or literary figure. I prefer to give credit to my mother, who would frequently say, "Trust all . . . but none too much," when I told her about situations in which I was let down by a person I had trusted. What she was really saying was to give everyone the benefit of the doubt, but be careful, and don't be surprised if a valued friend or colleague disappoints you.

This is perhaps a cynical approach, and there certainly are friends and colleagues whom you can trust. But it has been my experience that in a world where power and wealth are dominant factors in the lives of ambitious people, you can expect that some of your friends and colleagues will betray your trust if given the opportunity to advance themselves. If you have boundless faith in the people you have relationships with, and they turn on you, your surprise or mental anguish may prevent you from coping effectively with the situation. If you fully understand that betrayal can happen, you can put yourself in a better position to defend yourself or your actions.

Why should you trust people? Because nothing can be accomplished if there is no trust. You must put your trust in people or your organization will become paralyzed. If you really do trust people, and people believe that you trust them, they'll feel much more confident and much more a part of the organization. They will want to try to live up to that trust.

Most of your associates will substantiate your trust, but a few won't. If you are aware that there are some who will not be trustworthy, you won't be surprised, and your subconscious mind will be prepared to counter a failure of trust with alternative solutions.

Be Trustworthy

Make sure that people can depend on you.

While the phrase "Trust all . . . but none too much" can be an important weapon in your arsenal, it is vitally important for you to become absolutely trustworthy yourself. Being completely trustworthy will cause people to have faith in you and to come to depend on you, which is what you want if you are to succeed.

Being honest is a very important part of building trust, but becoming totally trustworthy goes beyond honesty. It means little things such as returning phone calls, meeting due dates on projects assigned to you, and following through on promises made. It also means giving credit to others for their ideas and, conversely, taking responsibility when things go wrong in areas for which you are responsible. It means doing your best to serve the interests of the people for whom you have responsibility.

Establishing a reputation for being trustworthy is an essential ingredient of leadership and building a successful career. We need only look at the political leadership in Washington today for examples of how not to build trust. Many of our political figures are not trusted by the people because their actions are primarily self-serving. Being interested in serving yourself first is the surest way to lose the trust of others.

A practical suggestion to make sure you follow up on promises is this: Use an effective organizing system. There are many good organizing systems available, from daily notebook-type organizers to sophisticated palm-held computers. One of America's most successful executives uses a system that's the height of simplicity: He writes the date at the top of an 8½-by-11-inch pad and then makes a list of pertinent issues he needs to follow up on. You don't necessarily have to spend hundreds of dollars or take all-day seminars to be effectively organized. You just have to find a system that works for you.

Make Judgments

Having opinions will enable you
to make contributions.

People who are considered judgmental are often
biased or overly critical to the point of being petty or
harsh. This is especially true when people make critical judgments about other people and express them to
whoever may listen.

While making harsh, outspoken judgments about
others is an undesirable trait, being able to judge, evaluate, or discern is necessary for survival in a business
career. If you don't make judgments or form opinions of
people as well as everything else you are exposed to,
you will not be a major contributor.

Having opinions does not mean that you should
become opinionated to the extent that you are not willing to listen or change your mind; but having opinions
will enable you to take positions on the myriad of issues
you face every day. You should become a judge or an
evaluator of anything or anyone that has some consequence to your business.

When evaluating your associates, measure their personalities, their talents, their experience, and their abilities
against yours. This may not sound "polite," but almost

everyone does this, even if only subliminally. Knowing the strengths and weaknesses of others is necessary in order to properly evaluate yourself, to discover what you need to do to improve.

As you progress in your career, you will make mistakes in judging people and situations. The important thing is to learn from these mistakes and not to let them hinder your progress with emotional letdowns.

How to Evaluate Yourself

Recognize your own worth
as soon as you can.

How do you stack up against your associates who are competing with you for advancement? You must measure their experience and how far they have progressed based on that experience. You must measure how well they think, how assertive they are, how articulate they are, whether they have natural charisma, whether they have good leadership qualities, how hard they work, whether they are honest and loyal, how they use the English language, and even their appearance and how they dress. And then you must do the same thing to yourself. You will probably stack up pretty well. More people underestimate themselves than overestimate themselves.

Realize that you are as good as and probably better than your associates at what you do.

Some have questioned this statement by pointing out that obviously not everyone can be the best at what they do. But I believe that a primary factor in accomplishing your goals is believing that you have the ability to do so.

I also believe that most people truly do not recognize their own worth. You must have confidence in your potential for success in order to succeed. This is the drive or ambition that gets people where they want to go, both in business and in other aspects of life. Realizing that you are as good as or better than your associates at what you do means recognizing and exercising your ability to improve upon your strengths, to eliminate your weaknesses, and to become as accomplished and capable as it is possible for you to be. Success is not just about raw skills or talent; self-confidence and determination make the difference between unrealized potential and fulfilled dreams. Realizing your own worth should change your life, in that you will recognize your talents and abilities and be better able to use them.

Quite often, recognizing your worth does not come until your mid-thirties or later. Try to recognize your value as early as possible in your career.

Charisma

Become charismatic.

Charisma is a rare, hard-to-explain human quality that favorably attracts other people. If you have charisma, your chances of becoming successful increase dramatically. Those who have charisma often don't recognize it in themselves. Perhaps the inability to recognize that one has charisma is part of its mystery. There may be relatively few people who have natural charisma, but I believe it is possible for anyone to become more charismatic and thereby enhance the opportunity for a more successful career.

I have heard it said that charisma is based on power and beauty. It seems to me, however, that it is largely a person's demeanor that makes one charismatic. Extremes in personality—too loud or too quiet, too demanding or not demanding enough, too rigid or overly casual—are not charismatic.

It is very difficult to change extremes in personality, but there are other things that can be done to become a more attractive or charismatic person. Listed below are some thoughts on developing charisma. Most of these suggestions are offered in other parts of this book. They cannot be repeated too often, however.

1. Become more genuinely caring, interested, and understanding in contacts with your associates.

This must be genuine, for if it isn't, people will know.

How do you become more genuinely caring? It is possible to become more caring—if you really want to. If you do not consider compassion to be an essential part of relating to other human beings, it will be difficult to develop your own compassionate nature. (You will probably do better in a job in which relating to people is not very important.)

Recognizing the authenticity of other people's problems is an important first step in becoming a truly caring person. In a way, this means creating an awareness in yourself that everyone else exists just as fully as you do. Your own perspective makes you seem to be the center of the universe, but in fact every person is the center of her or his own perspective.

If you do want to become a more genuinely interested person, realize that the problems that people bring to work with them are real. One thing that I would change in my career, if I could, would be to put more effort into the people of the corporations I worked for. While I believe I was able to show people that I cared, I feel in hindsight that I could have done a better job. I mention this because I am firmly convinced that if you take only one thing away from these writings it should be that if you keep the well-being of your people as the main focus of your efforts, you will be successful. When I say "your people," I mean anyone who has anything to do with the corporation, including employees, customers, and suppliers. To try to fill the needs of such a divergent group is often a difficult balancing act, but if you can accomplish this to a large degree, you will be successful in your career, regardless of the position you attain.

2. Caring for and interest in others can be demonstrated in many ways.

Probably the best way is to become a good and sympathetic listener. Many people become just plain rude when it is their turn to listen, and those who are doing the talking are the first to see this. While at times you may be bored to tears, the person doing the talking has a story to tell and likes you or respects you enough to tell it to you, and this should be respected. Just as important as listening is "following up" later on when you see a person who has confided in you. Ask how things are going!

3. Take an interest in others by remembering as much about them as you can.

Nothing is more flattering than remembering a new or seldom-seen colleague's name. Knowing about their families, especially their children, and their job prospects and responsibilities is extremely helpful if you want to connect with people.

4. Let people know that you think they are important.

Perhaps the best way is to ask questions on subjects in which they are interested. Ask questions about their health, their job, their hobbies, and their families. By doing this you will be able to convey to people that they are extremely important. Some leaders in business and politics are masters at making people feel that who they are and what they do is the first priority. This is an extremely effective way to build charisma.

5. Learn the names of your associates throughout the company and greet them with a smile and a friendly hello.

This becomes more important as you advance in an organization. I have seen companies with CEOs who are masters at this, and I've seen the opposite. While this is only one of the things that create an exciting, positive atmosphere in a company, you can definitely feel a difference in those companies where the CEOs are open and friendly with their people.

6. It is essential to be on a first-name basis with everyone, no matter how important your position.

I've been in companies where people who have worked alongside others for years still address each other as Mr. or Ms. This doesn't work. People like it when someone has taken the time to learn their first name, and they like it when they can address the boss by his or her first name.

Though it may be difficult to define charisma completely, I don't believe that "you either have it or you don't." You may think you do not have the inborn qualities that make a person charismatic, but if you practice the suggestions listed above, I am confident you will develop your own brand of charisma.

"If . . ."

All too often those who achieve success quickly forget where they came from.

T hose who achieve success often become isolated from the everyday things that are necessary to keep ideas flowing. I've seen many CEOs fail because they have surrounded themselves with their tremendous egos and staffs that support those egos to the detriment of the business.

While a strong ego is important to success, it is equally important to temper the ego from time to time so that you maintain "the common touch." Successful executives have different ways of doing this, but one way I have found that has been used by several CEOs is to learn, or at least read on occasion, the poem "If," by Rudyard Kipling. The poem is simplistic, and it reflects the gender biases of Kipling's time, but the advice is nonetheless valuable, whether you're a man or a woman. Frequent readings will help you remember not only to work on developing your personal strength, but to keep your ego in place. It is reprinted here. Memorize it or copy it, and keep it with you for frequent referrals.

If

If you can keep your head when all about you
    Are losing theirs and blaming it on you,
If you can trust yourself when all men doubt you,
    But make allowance for their doubting too;
If you can wait and not be tired by waiting,
    Or being lied about, don't deal in lies,
Or being hated, don't give way to hating,
    And yet don't look too good, nor talk too wise:

If you can dream—and not make dreams your master;
    If you can think—and not make thoughts your aim;
If you can meet with Triumph and Disaster
    And treat those two impostors just the same;
If you can bear to hear the truth you've spoken
    Twisted by knaves to make a trap for fools,
Or watch the things you gave your life to, broken,
    And stoop and build 'em up with worn-out tools:

If you can make one heap of all your winnings
    And risk it on one turn of pitch-and-toss,
And lose, and start again at your beginnings
    And never breathe a word about your loss;
If you can force your heart and nerve and sinew
    To serve your turn long after they are gone,
And so hold on when there is nothing in you
    Except the Will which says to them: "Hold on!"

If you can talk with crowds and keep your virtue,
    Or walk with Kings—nor lose the common touch,
If neither foes nor loving friends can hurt you,
    If all men count with you, but none too much;
If you can fill the unforgiving minute
    With sixty seconds' worth of distance run,
Yours is the Earth and everything that's in it,
    And—which is more—you'll be a Man, my son!

                    —Rudyard Kipling

Practical
Matters

High-Quality Thinking Skills

Developing your thinking skills
is of vital importance.

The lament heard most often from bosses is that their people do not know how to think. Honesty and taking responsibility are important, and being honest about your failures should not automatically get you in trouble, but there is a catch. If you have made a mistake because of poor thinking, or because you have not taken the time to think before you act, perhaps you should be in trouble!

The ability to think productively comes largely from your life experience. As you gain responsibility in your life and career, you will be expected to enlarge your ability to perceive a problem's true nature, to generate a number of possible solutions, to allow your subconscious mind to work on what you have generated, and to test and refine a solution or new idea in various ways. The larger your job, the greater also are the expectations of your coming up with new ideas and improving other thinking skills. A boss often quietly evaluates someone who has been given added responsibility by determining whether the person's thinking ability has kept pace with his or her new responsibilities. If you get caught several times not offering "good thinking" to a situation, you may find this is the quickest way for a career to come to a dead end. The people who succeed in a company are most often those who are good thinkers.

Your ability to think will be most readily apparent at the many meetings you will be asked to attend. Careers can be made or destroyed in meetings because of the complete exposure to bosses, peers, and subordinates. You will be evaluated by others, and if you show that you can make an intelligent analysis of a problem or generate ideas that demonstrate an understanding of the issue being discussed, you will be perceived as a contributor—even if the others are not completely aware that they are judging you on your "ability to think."

If you are new to the company or to a meeting, the best thing to do may be to remain quiet. But even if you are new, you may participate at an appropriate moment by asking an intelligent question that has been well prepared. Remember that you are treading on dangerous ground if the question shows too much naïveté.

Expose yourself to new information and procedures and you will acquire the raw material necessary for improving your thinking and problem-solving skills. A six-step problem-solving procedure ("Fixing Things"), which follows, will allow you to practice a number of basic thinking skills (seeing and articulating the true nature of a problem, making use of your general knowledge to generate ideas with "freewheeling" thought, relying on writing to develop and clarify your ideas, and even making use of your subconscious thinking). These six steps to solving a problem, which include testing your ideas by talking to other people, can guide the development of your ability to think and act productively.

Fixing Things

Six steps to a solution.

When things go wrong in a business, a typical management reaction is panic. It is unfortunate that many who are faced with a crisis approach it with fear and negative thoughts that cloud the mind and impair its ability to function. When a crisis develops, there may be one clear thinker who will develop a strategy to fix the problem. Such an individual is rare—but it is actually quite easy to become this clear thinker. Clear thinking and problem-solving (fixing things) can be learned. These six steps can help you become a solver of problems.

Step 1: Articulate the problem.

The problem must be clearly articulated. This means that you must go beneath the surface to get to the problem's true nature. All too often the reason given for a problem is incorrect because the issue has not been examined deeply enough.

Consider an example. A sales program for retail consumers does not seem to be working. The program is an in-store offer that allows customers to receive a discounted item by mail directly from the manufacturer after they have purchased two items in the store. The problem is that people are not responding to the offer. The managers assume that consumers are not buying the third item because they are not interested in the program.

A closer look at the program indicates that it is not the customers but the store personnel who do not like the program. Commissioned employees will not receive additional compensation because the customer must acquire the third item directly by mail from the manufacturer. Now the program can be altered to be attractive to store employees as well as to customers (perhaps by something as simple and obvious as offering the discount on an in-store item on which an employee can still make an extra commission).

Write down the nature of the problem. Once you discover the true nature of the problem, you can develop a plan to solve it.

Step 2: Write down your thoughts.

Allow your mind to "freewheel" with solutions. Write your thoughts as they occur. Let one thought follow another. Don't be concerned about how ridiculous some of the thoughts may be. This freewheeling process is important not only in solving problems but in developing instincts, developing vision, and making evaluations.

Step 3: Step away from the problem.

Stand back from the problem and let your subconscious mind work on it. If you try to develop a quick solution, you may later find it is not the best one. It is better not to offer a solution immediately, but to take twenty-four or forty-eight hours to think it through.

Step 4: Review your notes and come up with a solution.

After letting your subconscious mind work on the problem, review your notes; rewrite and edit them if necessary (this sometimes helps to clarify the issue). Then write down the steps that can be taken to solve or alleviate the problem. Make sure your solution is in a concise, clearly written form.

Step 5: Meet with two or three associates.

Present your associates with the proposed solution. Let them question your ideas. This meeting will be helpful, for you can be certain that your thoughts will be challenged. If you have followed the first four steps, you will probably be able to meet your associates' challenges. Often you will find that the challenges they present help you improve or enhance your solution.

Step 6: Finalize your solution.

Make your final presentation to the appropriate person or persons.

In most cases, these steps will lead you to a good solution.

A Freewheeling Thought Session

Consider a real-life example.

What follows is the unedited text of the notes I took when I sat down to think of an idea to improve Waldenbooks' share of the market in a stagnant economy. Freewheeling means just that. Do not worry about grammar or punctuation, and do not worry at this point about how other people will respond. Just get it down on paper.

How to improve our share of market in a stagnant economy—
Our competition is having the same problem. They do not appear to be doing anything really exciting to improve their business. How do we get the consumer to choose our store over theirs? We are both pretty much identical in attraction to the reader:

Location: Malls
Product: The same books
Service: Although we believe we're better, this may be intangible to the customer.
The real question is, How can we get customer loyalty?

How have other businesses done it? American Airlines

. . . The frequent flyer program really did a lot for American Airlines and their customers' loyalty. AA locked frequent flyers into making AA their first choice because of the added benefit of earning free flights. Competition followed, but AA was first. The one who is first will gain significantly from being first.

Why not develop a frequent-buyer program for our bookstores? What would such a program consist of? Can we afford it? Suppose we sign people up to a program for readers. When they buy a book from us, they would receive a discount as members of the program. They would need to fill out an application form.

We would need to assign a unique number to each member and collect their purchasing information so we could keep track of their buying preferences. Is a discount at purchase enough? Some of our competitors offer significantly higher discounts than we could afford.

What else does the program need? What does the customer want? The customer would like information on forthcoming books. We can provide that if we have their mailing address. We can also send mailings to those who have special category interests. As a lover of mysteries, I would like to receive a monthly magazine highlighting the new publications.

That's great, but what's to prevent the customer from taking the mailing to a discount store and buying the books? We really need some kind of hook that will offer a benefit to the customer to come back to our stores.

Frequent flyer programs accumulate mileage, notify customers on a monthly basis of how much they have accumulated, and then offer different types of programs the customer can use to cash in the accrued mileage. Can we offer a program that accumulates purchases over a period of time and that will offer a value to the customer when purchases reach a certain level? What if we were to give a coupon for x number of dollars when the customer buys $100 worth of product? What can we afford to give customers for their loyalty? We know from research that readers use several bookstores and that we usually get only a relatively small percentage of the entire yearly purchases of a reader. Will a 10 percent discount at purchase along with a $5 rebate on accumulated purchases be enough to gain the loyalty of a reader? I believe so, especially if we provide monthly information by mail. Can we afford the program? Can we charge for membership? How much? Is a yearly charge of $5 palatable to the reader? Is $10 too much? Initially I would think $5 is the right amount.

How do we sell the program? There should be very little cost involved, because the store people can sell it to every customer that comes to the cash wrap. Can we handle the programming? Do we have the computing capacity with our present equipment? Will the publishers help support the program with their co-op dollars?

After reviewing the above, I think we should consider the following:

1. Offer a Frequent Buyer program to all customers.
2. Customer pays $5 to join.

3. We give members a 10 percent discount on all purchases, including already-discounted items, plus an additional $5 coupon for every $100 in purchases over the entire year. Customer has to sign up each year and pay $5. Customer loses dollars that were accumulated if $100 is not reached, but we may use this as another incentive to sign up.
4. We should develop a monthly mailing program that provides targeted mailings to members based on their reading tastes.
5. Need to get publisher support.
6. Need to get in-house support.
7. Need to get store support.

Needless to say, a lot more work had to be done on the concept, including projections (guesses) and financial analysis of the projections. But the important thing to understand is that although there had been talk about frequent buyer programs in the book industry, it wasn't until the time was taken to perform the exercise above that a specific idea was developed to set the plan in motion. It took a freewheeling thought process to develop a concrete idea into a workable program that could be presented to others for development and refinement.

Anyone can try this type of freethinking, freewheeling process. It is relatively easy . . . all it takes is the discipline to sit down and not be afraid to write down what you are thinking.

This freewheeling session was the start of what turned out to be an extraordinarily successful program for Waldenbooks. By the end of the first year, over four million people had signed up for the program, which had become the "Preferred Reader" club. The club became the largest of its kind in the world. The opportunity to take advantage of the success of such a program is enormous for a company's future, if the key management of the company will sit down and go through a "freewheeling thinking process" to make the program better and more profitable.

Meetings

Participation can solve the problem
of the boring meeting.

Over the years I have heard many people complain about meetings—that they are too long and interrupt the flow of work being performed by the individual employee. Complaints about meetings are often valid. Unless the presenter is a great speaker with an exciting agenda, meetings can be interruptive and deadly boring, especially if the person conducting the meeting drones on and on about his or her agenda.

But meetings are essential.

I strongly believe that a meeting should require the participation of everyone present. The leader of the meeting must ensure that an agenda is set and that participants have enough time to prepare. It is important that the leader not allow those who are presenting a subject to "talk it to death." One method for preventing this is to gently interrupt in order to ask questions, or to ask someone else to comment on a statement the presenter has just made.

The leader should try to get a quick overview from all present of their thoughts on the subject being discussed. It is essential that those present understand that they are free to say whatever they please about the subject and that whatever is said will be evaluated fairly, even though it may not be what the leader or others want to hear. Allowing everyone to have this uninhibited say provides an opportunity to test the leader's own views against the views of others and to build a consensus agreement if possible. If the leader's position appears to be in the minority, and a consensus agreement is unlikely, allowing others to have their say will provide the leader the opportunity to either change his or her mind or answer the objections of the group.

Allowing others to participate (participative management) can be a very difficult way of managing. At times it will be necessary for a leader to make decisions that are not supported by the majority. But by at least giving others in the group an opportunity to speak without recrimination, many of the negative feelings that may come from an unpopular decision can be muted.

Know Thine Accomplishments

Keep track of what makes you
valuable to your company.

As you earn more responsibility in an organization, it
becomes essential that you constantly evaluate your
worth to the company. While in theory almost anyone is expendable, you probably have some talents or
abilities that would be difficult to replace. You need to
keep track of your accomplishments; this will help you
define any uniqueness you offer to the company. For
example, if you are in marketing and have a track record
of creating effective marketing programs, keep a record
of these programs and your contribution to them. If you
are responsible for purchasing supplies for the company
and supply costs have gone down, keep a record of your
purchasing decisions or methods. You may keep records
by entering your notes in a designated computer file, or
you can use the old tried-and-true, handwritten note-
book method.

There are several reasons for doing this. When review
time comes, you will be able to more effectively present
your case for an increase in salary or for more responsibility. Keeping a record will also give you protection
from those who have a penchant for stealing credit for

successful ideas and programs (these people do exist). A third reason for keeping a record of your accomplishments is that if you find your talents are not appreciated in your current job, you will be better prepared to present your achievements to companies who might appreciate them more.

Management by Objectives

MBO doesn't work—here's why.

For years "management by objectives" has been popular in the business world. While this type of management may be used in different ways by different companies, the basic concept is that a manager submits quarterly objectives to his or her boss. They then discuss these objectives and set up a quantitative method for measuring results at the end of the quarter. While this sounds like an excellent way to measure the effectiveness of a manager, I have always been skeptical of its value.

When I worked for a boss who used management by objectives, I spent an inordinate amount of time fretting over what I wanted to accomplish in the upcoming quarter as well as trying to account for the objectives we set for the current quarter. Often a new, equally important activity would divert my attention from previously established objectives.

The worst part of management by objectives is that it stifles creativity and inhibits a person's ability to respond quickly to the new challenges and opportunities that seem to occur every day in a company. If an organization insists on measuring performance by how many previously set objectives are actually accomplished, managers

85

are less likely to respond to new challenges and opportunities, thereby losing out on alternative chances for success. It is important for individuals to establish objectives, but these objectives can be long-range personal goals that can be discussed during an annual review.

I believe that a better way to set, measure, and meet goals, especially in our rapidly moving world, is by having short weekly departmental meetings where associates can discuss ongoing activities in the department. Simply going around the table and having people tell about the projects they are involved with is usually enough. These meetings let people in a department know what their associates are working on, and they enable the department to work more cohesively on current activities. Weekly departmental meetings also give the manager an opportunity to introduce new projects.

As CEO at Waldenbooks, I held a staff meeting with vice presidents and directors every Monday morning. We simply went around the table and reported on sales for the past week, the outlook for upcoming weeks, the financial situation of the company, and any special activities in marketing, MIS (management information systems), or other departments. I found these meetings to be very helpful in setting objectives for the upcoming weeks and months. As each described his or her accomplishments, I had an opportunity to review the performance of the various managers. Many of the innovative activities Waldenbooks became known for were born in these meetings, often in response to a problem that arose during the meeting or in response to our learning of some new activity of our competitors.

One Hour a Day . . .

Get in shape and stay in shape.

You can have the best education, be smarter than most, even be the best at what you do, but if you are not physically fit, your opportunity for growth may be limited. Staying in good shape is as important as anything you do. It is important to your health. It is important to your psyche. If you are in good shape, you will be able to attack difficult tasks with vigor. If you are in good shape, you will make a favorable impression on those with whom you work, even though it may be subliminal. You will feel better about yourself and feel more confident in your dealings with others.

Getting in shape and staying in shape is not difficult if you are willing to dedicate an hour a day to your body. It is the least you can do to preserve such a wonderful structure. If you are willing to devote this hour a day, the positive returns will surpass those of almost any other hour-long activity you engage in.

There are many excellent books and magazines that can help you develop a suitable physical fitness program, but the two simplest, least costly, and easiest things to do are to walk or jog and to perform strength training with weights. Jogging for a half hour a day four or five times a week will keep you aerobically fit. Even doing a shuffle jog, taking small steps with your feet barely off the ground, will do the job; you won't do as much distance, but you will start to perspire and breathe hard. A half hour with ten-, fifteen-, or twenty-pound dumbbells—or even three- or five-pound dumbbells—three times a week will keep your body toned, and you will find that your strength increases dramatically.

Being fit is a major asset as you work toward your career goals. As you advance in your career you probably will spend more of your time working, as much as sixty or seventy hours a week. Even with this increased demand on your time, you must find the time to work out.

Integrity

Honesty

Use a simple phrase to test your actions.

As your career advances you will find that your basic values are constantly challenged. There will be times when all the good things your mother taught you are tested by an opportunistic society that seems to reward those who conduct their businesses and their lives by the familiar tenet that the end justifies the means—and the "end" is usually the self-interest of those who live by this philosophy.

There will always be a few who are able to fool the system—to "get away" with not doing their work, or to acquire money or power through theft or dishonesty. But you need only look at the political tragedies of the '70s and the business tragedies of the '80s to see that greed and dishonesty do not pay in the long run, and that many of the mighty will fall. Acting dishonestly just isn't worth it. No matter what you end up doing in your business life, you need to adhere to this form of the Golden Rule: Be honest with yourself, and be as honest with others as you are with yourself.

One of the best ways to ensure your integrity is to develop an honesty check in the form of a phrase that you can use to test your decisions. A simple phrase I have used over the years is "What's right, and what's fair?" As I encountered situations that required decisions affecting an individual or the company, I always tested my decision with that phrase. It is a useful phrase, because so many of your decisions must be based on turning a profit that it is sometimes easy to forget that there are other factors to consider. Make yourself stop from time to time, to examine your priorities.

Of course, conflicting values arise constantly in business, and you must serve as a judge. With the help of your honesty check, you must try to be an objective judge, no matter how you or your company may be affected by your decision.

You must be honest not only in your business dealings, but also in your emotional dealings with the people you work with. Developing an honesty check is especially important when you are dealing with employees. It is vital that you develop trusting relationships by giving credit for ideas and accomplishments to those who are responsible for them.

Taking Responsibility

Owning up to decisions gone wrong
will pay off in the long run.

You must take responsibility for what you do. There
will be times when decisions you make will turn
out badly, or you may not be able to live up to your
commitments. You must be frank with your boss when
discussing your failings and mistakes. You will find that
a good boss would much rather hear the truth than hear
an effort to "cover up."

Taking responsibility for your actions that turn out
badly is certainly one of the most difficult things a person can do. Somewhere in the human psyche is a self-
preserving voice that tries to rationalize an error or put
blame on something or someone else. Answer this
voice's attempt to escape responsibility with the phrase
"What's right, and what's fair?" Is it really true that the
art director "completely ruined the brochure," or is it
more fair to admit that you did not give this person all
the necessary information? If you make a bad decision,
will it really help your standing in others' eyes to blame
the decision on "those incompetent people in accounting"? If you do not take responsibility for your actions,

it may appear on the surface that a situation has been smoothed over, but those who have been unfairly blamed will not forget what happened.

In the long run, a responsible attitude will pay off. People will respect you for being scrupulous and, more important, you will have your self-respect.

Fooling the System

Appearing to be an asset to the company is not the same as being an asset.

A regional sales manager at one of the companies I worked for went into the telephone room every morning, put a newspaper over his face, and slept for much of the day. He was able to "get away" with this because he did the minimum work required to stay in touch with his salespeople by telephone—but he certainly was not making an important contribution to the company.

Another regional manager at another company never made sales calls or worked with the salespeople. He seemed to think that his job was entertaining the spouses of his associates.

Both of these people kept their jobs for many years, and they may have felt some satisfaction that they were able to "fool the system." This approach to work will appeal only to those persons who believe that the perception of accomplishment is as good as real accomplishment, and who will not be troubled by a conscience reminding them that they are benefiting from the hard work of other people. You are not such a person.

Commitment

Establish your reputation as someone who can be counted on.

L earn to recognize when you have made a commitment. Honor it even when it appears it may have a negative impact.

Of course, you should feel free to try to renegotiate a settlement that is fair to all when new information or further reflection indicates that an original commitment may be unfair, or if a condition has changed dramatically. For example, if you find you are providing additional services to a customer, you may try to get a better discount or better terms for your agreement.

You can use your honesty check ("What's right, and what's fair?") when evaluating a commitment. Perhaps a salesperson has made a commitment to a customer, has promised something that the salesperson later finds out is against company policy. He or she may discuss this with the boss, and both may ask what is right and what is fair. Perhaps they decide that because the salesperson made a commitment to a customer they will have to abide by that commitment, even though it is against company policy. Perhaps they will determine that it really would not be fair (perhaps to other customers or to other people in the company), and that the salesperson will have to explain to the customer what has happened.

No matter how trivial they may be, it is important to follow through on obligations and promises. Returning phone calls, filing reports, showing up for meetings, and keeping appointments on time are all part of keeping your commitments and establishing your reputation as someone who can be counted on. This will help build an atmosphere of trust in your company and diminish a culture of fear.

Even more important, be careful not to make more commitments than you can keep. Those you make and keep will have a lot of value; those you make and do not keep will have no value beyond a brief "feel good" moment.

Be aware that a friendly comment you say casually to an employee ("You'll be going to the trade shows this year") may be taken very seriously by that employee, to the extent that he or she rearranges schedules and family plans. It would be better to say, "If sales keep up the way they are now, I will talk to you about your going to the trade shows this year."

Failure: Your Own

Learning from a mistake will allow
you to put it behind you.

One of the most difficult things to come to grips
with is failure. Failure can lead to a complete break-
down of one's self-esteem, even to intense depres-
sion. But the truth is that everyone makes mistakes. In
your career, failure can occur when trying to meet the
expectations of your boss, your subordinates, or even
yourself. Coping with failure is difficult, but if you really
want to grow, you must be able to learn something from
a failure and then put it behind you.

During my first year as the head of a small book
wholesaling company that was struggling for survival, I
read about a company called Vinabind. This company's
primary business was stripping the front and back covers
of published paperback books, then reattaching them
with a cardboard and laminating process—essentially
making a hardcover book.

I thought this was a great idea. Some of our best customers at the time were libraries. Their buyers were
reluctant to buy paperbacks because they were fragile
and had a short life span. I believed that I had found the

answer to increasing sales to libraries by making paperbacks into hardbacks with the Vinabind process.

I called the Vinabind people, met with them, and set
up a program to turn paperback books into hardcover
books. And we did that—by the thousands. The problem
was that the libraries didn't buy them. The reason,
whether it was the upcharge for the books or that the
librarians didn't like dealing with a smaller hardcover edition, didn't really matter. I had failed in one of my first
efforts to bring an innovative idea into the book business. Thousands of dollars that we could ill afford were
wasted, as well as a great deal of time and effort.

Beyond the time and cost, my own confidence could
have been seriously impaired to the extent that I would
not be willing to try other new ideas in the future.
Fortunately, I was able to convince myself that I had
learned a lot from this failure, and that the next big idea
would benefit from what I had learned.

Certainly the most important lesson I learned was
that you should always investigate to find out if the customer has any interest in a new idea. In order to bring
innovation and ideas to your company, you must be a
risk taker, but you must also make sure that you have
exposed your idea or plan to intensive thought and
research. Instincts play an important role when deciding
to implement an idea, but if you have not also developed a well-thought-out plan, the tolerance for your failures will diminish.

Taking responsibility for your failures is a very difficult thing to do, but when you do, you will find that a
couple of positive things happen. In most cases your

failure will be tolerated, and you might even be given credit for trying. Taking responsibility for your own failure will also earn the trust of those around you.

I found people to be understanding of my mistake. I believe they felt encouraged to take chances themselves because they knew that if they were to fail in some endeavor, they would not be chastised or penalized.

Failure: Of Others

Allow your associates to act without fear.

If you as a boss do not handle the failures of your people in a proper manner, you will never be able to bring out the best in them. The most important reason for a company's success is that the people in the company are able to act without fear. The proper way to respond to the failure of another may have more to do with what you *avoid* doing than with what you actually *do*. It is most important to avoid blaming or punishing looks or remarks. You will then be able to see how the person him- or herself deals with the failure. Does the person recognize what has happened? Does he or she appear to have learned from it?

Of course, this gentle approach is the right one for "well-intentioned failures." Failures that result from actions taken to damage or undermine the company need not be tolerated.

But if the management of a company develops a reputation for automatically blaming and punishing employees when things go wrong, an atmosphere of fear will grow and the company itself will become a candidate for failure.

Your Machiavellian Side

The Prince by Niccolo Machiavelli should be required reading for anyone who wants to enter the world of business or politics.

Machiavelli's work has been interpreted and evaluated in many different ways. Many have praised the author for his assessment of reality ("realpolitik"). Many others consider his work to be evil. One definition of Machiavellian in *Merriam-Webster's Collegiate Dictionary,* tenth edition, is "marked by cunning, duplicity, or bad faith." The phrase often associated with Machiavelli's philosophy is "The end justifies the means." I dislike this saying, especially when it is used to justify unethical, illegal, or destructive behavior.

But there are things that even a person of goodwill can learn from reading Machiavelli. Even the person who genuinely respects and cares about people may at times have to take actions just because they need to be taken, not because everyone else is happy about them. And it may sometimes be necessary to manipulate people, even to "play on their feelings," in order to get something important accomplished. Even the "good person" must recognize that *everyone* has a "Machiavellian" side. You must be willing to make use of this part of your personality to be successful in the corporate world.

Your style may be to listen to the opinions of all and to get consensus on major decisions, but this is not always possible. Perhaps you are a manager who has spent several fruitless hours in a meeting trying to persuade your associates of the rightness of a course of action that you believe will be good for the company and its people in the long run. Most of the group gets up to go to lunch, leaving you in the meeting room with two of your associates who have supported you during the discussion. Perhaps you look at the other two and say: "Let's just do it. Let's do it while they're at lunch."

Another thing we can learn from Machiavelli is to take advantage of opportunities that unexpectedly present themselves. Something you learn by accident may turn out to be valuable information. You should be prepared to discuss your ideas and plans at unexpected opportunities. Such a time may be a social occasion at which a key figure in your company is present or any occasion at which you unexpectedly run into a person you have been wanting to present with your ideas. These times will occur, and you must be prepared to take advantage of them.

At times it may seem prudent not to take an action that you believe is right because you also have a fear that there is a chance you may be wrong. But if you feel strongly enough about what to do in a given situation: Do it.

The Good
Boss

Authority Figures

Power does not always mean competence.

For the first thirty years of my life I had a great deal of difficulty dealing with authority figures. Certainly shyness and a lack of self-confidence contributed to my inability to deal with people in power. But the main reason for my difficulty was that, like most American children of that day, I was brought up to have complete and trusting faith in those who were in positions of power.

Those in authority often have a protective instinct that motivates them to fend off challenges to their power. They quickly learn of the existence of this faith in the powerful, and they learn how to keep their power by keeping the less powerful in line. This strong protective instinct will sometimes allow people to remain in power no matter how badly they perform.

Though fewer children today are brought up with the blind faith in the powerful common to my generation, it is still common to be overawed by a person's powerful position. Although it is a good idea to show respect to everyone, it is also good to be aware that power does not always mean competence.

Shyness and lack of confidence are not easy things to

overcome, but the most difficult obstacle to surmount in a quest for success is having to work for an inept boss. Many inept bosses are inept simply because they are constantly striving to hold and improve their power base. While engaging in this struggle, they often forget their real purpose, which is to improve the operation or function for which they are responsible, as well as to bring out the best in their people.

On Being a Good Boss

Even brilliant managers with extraordinary vision cannot be assured of success unless they have people who support them.

Most self-help books for managers offer ways to advance your career by providing information on the problems of career growth, handling bosses, holding effective meetings, and other such issues. These books may discuss strategies for dealing with subordinates, but they often focus on the negative elements of handling people. Very little attention is given to the topic of how to be a good boss—*which may be the most important factor in developing a successful career.*

As a manager, your first concern must be your people, and you must give top priority to providing them with a working environment that gives them satisfaction and a love for what they do.

Developing innovative programs, knowing the market, communicating goals, and making use of people's skills and talents are important managerial responsibilities. But it is most important to empower people and show caring. On the next few pages I will address these two often-neglected issues, and offer suggestions to help you become a better boss.

Empowerment

Everybody needs some power.

You may be partially successful in bringing out your people's best by keeping tight control over their activities and by constantly supervising their performance. In the long run, this won't work.

People are more likely to do a good job when they know why they are doing it, and when they clearly understand the company's goals. You must empower your people and give them an opportunity to succeed or fail on their own.

You must give your people an idea of what you and the company are trying to accomplish, and then let them develop ways to reach these goals. This does not mean that you will not know what is going on—you must always have a strong sense of what your area of responsibility is producing. But you are more likely to know what is going on when you communicate openly with your people about company goals and situations. They will then naturally want to communicate freely with you.

Everyone wants some power. The boss who insists on making every single decision, no matter how small, is robbing employees of the chance to reach their full potential.

When I began working at Waldenbooks, we constantly sent out dictates from the home office concerning proper handling of cash, inventory, purchasing regulations, and other procedures. It seemed we were afraid the people in the stores would not comply with all our regulations; we were not trusting them to do the right things.

Finally I saw this wasn't working very well. There were too many regulations they had to follow (one compliance form had a list of 120 things to do). When I talked to the people who worked in the stores, they said they wanted to take some risks. We told them we would come out with guidelines from the home office, "but if they don't work for you, don't do them." This increased the atmosphere of trust in the company—and we discovered that the people in the stores would usually find ways of doing things better than what the home office came up with.

Showing Caring

Motivate people the best way.

Often the more responsibility a person acquires, the less effort that person puts into showing caring. Becoming a "boss" seems to carry with it an invitation to become domineering, someone to be feared. If you think it is your responsibility as a boss to show who is in charge by being a tyrant, you are wrong. This may be the style of certain despotic companies (see "Understanding Corporate Culture," Type 2, page 10), but there tends to be a very high turnover in such companies. If your style is tyrannical, you should be aware that there are high costs associated with this style (high turnover, lack of creativity, lack of trust). Your people will suffer, and so will your company. Are you willing to pay these costs?

The best way to encourage people to become responsive and responsible is to be a boss who shows that he or she genuinely cares about people. This effort to display caring should actually *increase* as you make your way up the corporate ladder. As you acquire more power, your words and actions will affect more people in the company, and you will have a greater responsibility for the atmosphere of the company. The most important rule is to treat everyone the way you would like to be treated, and this is usually with recognition, kindness, and understanding.

It may be the smallest nuances that make the biggest and longest-lasting favorable impressions. Greet people while walking through the halls at work with a smile and a "hello." Learn the names of those who work with you. Be aware of people's accomplishments and of the interesting things they are doing in and out of the office, so that you can mention these things at appropriate times.

It has been a source of cynical amusement to me to see how many people have become invisible to a newly pro-moted vice president making his or her way through the halls! Try to be on a first-name basis with everyone who works for you, regardless of your position. And make yourself available to those who seek your counsel.

These acts must be genuine. If you are performing them only to make a favorable impression, people will know. If you are doing them because you really care, peo-ple will know that, too. (See "Charisma," page 61.)

Listening

Become a good listener.

Being a good listener is important in developing a career. If you are a leader who has a reputation for being a good listener, people will come to you more often with ideas, and many of them will be good ideas.

Listening is sometimes difficult because much of what you hear can be very boring. But even a person you find boring can have something to say that might be of value to the company. Even if the person has nothing of great value to contribute at that moment, try to remember that maintaining a positive relationship is always valuable.

A person is often quite nervous about approaching the boss with an idea. You will show by your body language and the expression on your face if you are taking in what the other person is saying. If you appear disinterested or impatient, the employee will leave your office feeling bad, and will probably form (and broadcast) a bad opinion of you. Be an interested person—and show it.

Perception

How you are perceived by others can partially determine your business success.

Whether you are a boss, a peer, or a subordinate, people will develop a perception of how you relate to others. If they believe you relate well to people, they will like you. If they believe you are standoffish, they will have neutral feelings about you, or perhaps even dislike you. And if your face shows anger and hostility, they will fear you as well as dislike you.

Usually these perceptions are just that—perceptions— and they have very little to do with the kind of person you really are. But if people's thoughts about you are neutral, or if they fear or dislike you, it can badly hurt your career.

Analyze yourself to determine if you really do care about people. If you don't, you should take stock of what you are doing. If your job requires working with people, you should seriously consider changing careers and getting into a line of work in which interaction with people is minimal. If you have performed your self-evaluation and have determined that you really like people and enjoy associating with them, then it becomes easy to create a favorable impression and you don't have to spend a lot of time or effort on it.

Be aware that as you acquire more power, more eyes will be on you. Sometimes people will see things in your expression that aren't really there. For example, an unsmiling look may be interpreted as anger, and it may engender fear in other people. It's usually a good idea for a boss to maintain a smile—unless there is good reason not to.

Handling Conflicts between Employees

It is not always clear who is right
and who is wrong.

If you are a manager who has more than one person reporting to you, there will undoubtedly be times when conflicts arise between members of your organization. Those who are having a problem may come to you, each expecting you to take his or her side and to solve the problem by chastising the other party.

Most of the time it is not absolutely clear who is right and who is wrong. If one person comes to you, you will have to get the other party's view of the situation, and this is often difficult to do. By taking the subject of the conflict to this second person, it may seem as if you are either accusing this person or taking sides.

The best way to handle a conflict is to meet with both parties at the same time and let them talk it out. Start the meeting on a positive note by stating that each individual is important to the department and the company. Then say your intention is to be a listener and that you expect "two smart people" to be able to work the problem out without your interfering—but if they can't, you will. Then set ground rules. The most important ground rule is that each party have the opportunity to tell his or her story without interruption. After each party has presented his or her case, you may have to become the arbiter, but it is better if you don't. I have found in most cases a satisfactory resolution will be made if there is a threat of taking the decision out of their hands.

Most conflicts in an organization originate as personality differences. It is often impossible to change how a person feels about a different personality type, but it isn't really important for the people in your organization to like one another as long as they maintain the proper decorum in their everyday relationships. In fact, some conflict can be healthy—it sets up a competitiveness that brings new ideas and approaches to the company. The key is to not let a conflict get out of hand so that it damages the department or the company.

The Annual Review

Put yearly reviews in the hands of
the people being reviewed.

Reviews are often used for career advancement, for developing programs for self-improvement to assist those who are having difficulty on the job, or for putting an underperforming person on warning. Most of the time, neither reviewer nor reviewee looks forward to an annual review. While an employee's performance may have been stellar over the past year, it is often very difficult for a manager to prepare a traditional review that captures the major positive and negative aspects of that performance. It is also a difficult process for the person being reviewed, because the person may not feel sure that his or her performance is fully recognized. A review can be almost meaningless unless there has been a significant achievement (or failure) on the part of the reviewee. At times I have observed that unscrupulous reviewers are not entirely objective and may allow their like or dislike of an individual to affect the review.

At Waldenbooks we tried a different approach to annual reviews that significantly eased the trauma of review time and gave a more accurate picture of a person's performance. We set up a program of self-review, in which employees were given a simple form to fill out. They were asked to write down their accomplishments over the past review period as well as the areas in which they would like to see themselves improve. At the end of the self-review, employees were asked to rate themselves for the review period on a scale of one to one hundred, one hundred being optimum. The review was then submitted to the reviewer and the human resources department, and a time was set for discussion. Before the meeting, the reviewer went over the self-review and completed a similar form, commenting on the employee's achievements and areas needing improvement. The manager also rated the employee on the same scale the employee had used to rate him- or herself.

This type of review accomplished several things. It greatly simplified the reviewer's task, because he or she no longer had to spend a large amount of time trying to remember all the positive and negative aspects of an employee's performance. It also provided the reviewee with an opportunity to fairly present his or her accomplishments, as well as to openly discuss areas for improvement.

When we first introduced the self-review, there was a considerable amount of skepticism about how honestly the person being reviewed would perform a self-evaluation. As it turned out, most employees understated their performance as well as their numerical evaluation, and were often upgraded by the reviewer.

I believe that the self-review program had a lot to do with the positive attitude that prevailed at Waldenbooks. It added dignity and a more honest approach to the review process, which had been abused in the past.

When You Must Take Negative Action

Sometimes negative action is necessary.

Gaining the trust of others is an important part of your career development, but there are times in a business when it may be necessary for you to take negative action against an associate. These times occur when an associate's conduct is causing harm to the business or to other associates within the business. Taking negative action is always a difficult thing to do, but it is sometimes essential that it be done—and it must be done right, with a complete understanding of the situation.

Negative conduct can range from theft to lying to treating people badly to complete incompetence. Each situation may be handled in a number of different ways, but if the knowledge of the problem is yours, it becomes your responsibility to do something about it. You must be accurate in your understanding of how the associate is negatively affecting the business. Then come up with a way to handle the situation. Sometimes the only solution is termination, but don't be too hasty to fire someone.

It may be possible to approach the offender and discuss the situation. This is a desirable approach if the person has made a significant contribution over the years and deserves counseling because of that contribution. But be aware that this approach can be filled with jeopardy. It is likely that the person will deny any type of misconduct, and you may face the threat of retaliation.

Another approach is to discuss the situation with others you trust. (Remember, trust all, but none too much.) If you can get support and insight or counsel from others, it will be much easier to come up with a solution to the problem.

While theft and lying or falsifying information are difficult issues to deal with, the most difficult problem to handle may be incompetence. It is necessary to dismiss people who are incompetent, because incompetence can be damaging to the rest of the people in the organization and to the organization as a whole. This action can be difficult in part because your perception of incompetence may be different from the perceptions of others, especially of the person in question. A person you perceive as incompetent may instead be completely "burned out" or in the midst of personal difficulties that make it difficult to remain focused. If this is the case, counseling may have the most positive effect and may be the best course of action.

Termination

The reason a person has failed in a job will affect how you handle the termination.

One of the most difficult and distasteful jobs a manager has is terminating the employment of an associate. It is never easy, even when there is just cause. The person being terminated will suffer humiliation as well as fear and anxiety about where to find another job and how he or she will manage without an income until the next job is found.

A company and its managers bear a significant amount of the blame for a termination due to poor performance, and this should be taken into consideration when a termination package is being prepared. It is my belief that when a person fails in a job, it is usually for one of four basic reasons:

The first reason is that the hiring process may not have been thorough enough and the person was underqualified—this is management's fault.

The second reason a person may fail in a job is that he or she was not adequately trained—again, management's fault.

The third reason is that during the hiring process inadequate attention may have been given to whether or not the prospective employee would fit into the culture of the company. For example, the management style of a company may be autocratic and the prospective employee, though talented, may just not fit into an autocratic culture. Once again, this is the fault of management.

The fourth reason a person may fail in a job is that the person, although qualified, well trained, and compatible with a company's culture, is just not "into" working, lacks good judgment, or perhaps doesn't like the job. While this fourth reason should perhaps have come to light in the preemployment interviews, it is usually difficult to be absolutely sure the prospective employee has "the right stuff." Of course, theft and other unethical behaviors are obvious reasons for termination, and I would place these in this fourth category as well.

If management takes responsibility for the failure of the employee, a termination package based on one of the first three reasons for termination should be more generous than one based on the fourth reason. Compensation over a longer period than established by policy, outplacement services, and extended medical benefits should all be considered when determining how to ease the blow of termination for someone who has been inexpertly hired but may have worked hard for the company. Company policy is adequate procedure for an employee who has been terminated for the fourth reason (that is, he or she has an inadequate work ethic, does not like the job, or has demonstrated unethical behavior).

The termination meeting should be kept simple. There should be previous warnings about poor performance in the individual's file. Chances are good that the employee is expecting the worst. In cases where management bears some of the responsibility, it is important that you try to ease the pain of termination. One way to do this is to let the person know that while he or she has many good qualities, a company with a different culture would probably provide a better working environment for him or her. (This is not to suggest that the culture of a company should be so hidebound that there is no room for dissidence.) Letting employees go because they do not fit into the culture of a company is a gentler method of termination than presenting a list of the employee's deficiencies, and an inability to understand or fit into the culture of a company is indeed the reason many people fail. A person will probably accept this more readily than other reasons you may give.

Isolated Bosses

Many executives come up from the ranks but seem to forget quickly what life was like before their promotions—and they forget how they felt about bosses who isolated themselves.

Empowering your people and giving them the opportunity to make mistakes should be an important part of your management style, but you should also be available to help fix things.

No matter how big your office is, keep your door open and let people know that you are available. There will, of course, be times when you need to close the door for private meetings and even for short times to escape the hourly pressures of business. But if you keep the door closed most of the time, your people will begin to believe that you are operating in a constant crisis situation, or that you are completely uninterested in them.

When one becomes an executive, perks may kick in that have a tendency to take a new executive out of the mainstream and into an area that is primarily for bosses. Executive dining rooms and executive floors in office buildings are two of the most telling indicators that as people get promotions they become more and more isolated. While the rationale of an executive dining room may appear sound—in that it allows the bosses to sit down and discuss business—it would be of far greater advantage to them and to the company if they would go into the cafeteria and sit with the people to learn about what is really going on in the company. Executive floors in office buildings are huge mistakes. They become escapist sanctuaries for those responsible for running the company and places of fear and intimidation for employees.

Executives should be with the people for whom they are responsible. As you advance in management, do everything in your power to stay with the people.

On
Leadership

Cynicism in the Workplace

Layoffs should be a last resort.

Many people who work today's enterprises believe they are being used as pawns for the advancement and well-being of management. Cynicism prevails in the workplace because CEOs sometimes take care of themselves financially while ordering massive layoffs to appease the board of directors and Wall Street. Business leaders have succumbed to the pressures of the stock market for short-term results. They have become so obsessed with the power their positions give them that they will do whatever is necessary to preserve that power, often at the expense of employees and the enterprise itself.

If it is necessary to preserve an enterprise through massive layoffs, it is usually the managers who have failed, and the managers should be held accountable. A failing business is often the consequence of management by people who have not provided the necessary leadership and caring to keep a company ahead of the times.

If you as a manager find yourself in the position of having to help save a company in trouble, try following the advice given in the rest of this book before resorting to massive layoffs.

The Most Important Rule of Leadership

As a leader you must provide the vision, the environment, and the sense of urgency that will encourage imaginations to consistently improve and add value to the products and services of your business.

This must be the primary rule for all those who are leaders or who aspire to leadership. You must continually, *and always with a sense of urgency*, add value to the product or service that you're selling. Whether you are selling services or manufacturing widgets, your product can never rest on its laurels. There must always be something in development that will lead to improvement in the services offered or improvement in the function of the product being built. This is the responsibility of all the leaders in the enterprise, not just the CEO or the executive committee.

Improving Your Business

Ask yourself a question.

I believe that I could go into any company in America and, after spending a few weeks observing their business, make suggestions regarding the products and services they offer that would improve their sales by at least 5 to 10 percent. It's not that I am extraordinarily smart or talented. It's just that I have learned over the years to view the products and services offered by companies as a consumer, and I view them critically in terms of what would make them more appealing to me.

Fortunately, my views as a consumer are the same as those of many consumers. I built a career by articulating how the products and services offered by the companies I worked for could be improved so that they would be more appealing to me and better serve my needs (and therefore be more appealing to and better serve the needs of our customers). I always asked myself the question, "What can we do that would make it easier for customers to buy the products and services we offer?" Often the answer could be found in something nobody else was doing.

In the early 1970s, I was a senior manager at a small book wholesaler in Nashville, Tennessee. We were doing

133

modestly well, wholesaling books to schools and libraries as well as to a few local retail stores. But the growth of our business seemed to me to be inordinately slow, and I kept asking myself what were the needs of our customers and how could we serve them better than others were doing. By asking the question and observing how retail bookstores were supplied their books, I came to the conclusion that retailers were terribly underserved by their suppliers, publishers, and local independent book distributors.

Publishers were slow in shipping orders, taking up to three to five weeks for delivery. While independent distributors supplied their customers much more rapidly, the discounts they offered were minuscule. Viewing the situation as a customer, it seemed to me the situation was intolerable and had been so for many years. If I were a book retailer, why couldn't I get orders shipped at once from the publishers? While I never fully understood the answer to this question, I believed that my company could change things for book retailers and get orders shipped at once. We had a warehouse with books, we had telephones to take orders, and we had dedicated people who would make sure any order that was called in before 10 A.M. would be shipped the same day. All other orders would be shipped within twenty-four hours, at discounts that were reasonable.

This was a very simple, customer-oriented idea. But the idea worked, and the company became the largest wholesaler of books to retail bookstores in the United States.

While the company was growing as a result of this idea, we were always trying to improve on the basic idea, looking as a customer might at what we were doing. The years saw many improvements that kept the company in position as the number one book wholesaler in the country.

While this example illustrates how a simple idea became enormous in size, there were many much smaller ideas that were generated because everyone in the company tried to think as a customer.

Today, I am still the ultimate consumer. I constantly think in terms of how products or services could be improved to make them more valuable to me as a consumer. It may be little things such as painting the worn wall of a retail store where I shop, or toning down a cacophonous TV commercial that turns me, and many others, off. Perhaps the first thing I see when walking into a store is a large NO CHECKS ACCEPTED sign. This means a potential customer is being hit with a negative greeting before he or she sees anything else! Perhaps a doughnut shop has paper on the floor, or the restrooms in a discount store are not clean. Perhaps a sales catalog has tiny pictures that make it difficult for a customer to get a clear idea of what the products are like. All these things can be changed, are very easy to change, and can make a big difference to the customer.

Any of us can do this if we think about our own reactions to what we see and hear from the companies that are trying to get our business. If you become a constructive critic of the products and services offered by your own company, and if you are able to develop ways to improve on the products and services, you will have a distinct advantage over those who don't.

Put Yourself in the Customer's Shoes

You must get to know your customer's business and needs intimately.

In 1972, when computerization was still in its infancy, I was running a small wholesaling company that sold books to retail bookstores by telephone. Our biggest challenge was how to present to the bookstores an up-to-date catalog of the thousands of titles our company had in the warehouse. Obtaining up-to-date information was a major problem for all retailers in the book industry because of the immense numbers in publishing and because of the volatility of the industry. Wholesalers had tried traditional catalogs, but creating a catalog of thousands of titles was expensive, and the information became outdated very quickly. But the fact remained that bookstores needed up-to-date information in order to do their business efficiently and to make good ordering decisions.

One day while visiting a publisher in New York, I was asked by the publisher's vice president of finance if I would like to see the new accounts payable system he had just installed. To broaden my knowledge, I reviewed the system and found that it used computer-generated microfiche, on which could be listed thousands of the publisher's customers on a machine-readable 4-by-6-inch film. I learned that the film, microfiche, was easily and quickly produced, that it was inexpensive, and that it could be read quickly. All that was required was to insert the film in the tray of an inexpensive microfiche reader to enlarge the information to a readable type size. I began to think this could be the answer to the industrywide problem of presenting a timely catalog of thousands of titles to retail bookstores.

On returning to my hotel room, I immediately began to write down what I had learned microfiche could do and came up with the basic idea of listing twenty thousand book titles on microfiche to be sent out to retail stores every week.

That week I began trying to get help from the manufacturers of microfiche readers to develop my idea. I approached three large companies and was unable to elicit any interest. Finally I made a call to the CEO of one of the companies, who happened to be a personal friend. Within sixty days the company developed a reader that would enable a customer to read the microfiche sent by the book wholesaler every week, listing all twenty thousand titles with the quantities the wholesaler had on hand in the warehouse and on order.

It seemed like a good idea. But there was a problem. The bookstore that received the microfiche needed to have a microfiche reader in order to make use of the information. Microfiche readers cost about $125. It was difficult to believe that a retail bookstore would spend the money necessary to buy a reader. Even the microfiche itself, though inexpensive to produce, did have a cost, and so did postage. I was beginning to think my company could not afford this idea.

Again, I put myself in the shoes of the customer (the book retailer) and came to the conclusion that the program was so good that a retailer could not turn it down— if the cost of the program could be made fairly easy for the retailer to absorb. How? A lease program would make microfiche affordable for the retailer, and would allow the wholesaler to retain ownership of the reader. At the same time, the lease payments would enable the wholesaler to recover the cost of the machine and of the production of the weekly microfiche.

Then came the test. Would the retailer buy the program? Armed with a reader and a newly produced microfiche, I went to see my largest, toughest, and most important customer. I presented the concept and showed the program to the buyer. This was the buyer's response: "You're asking me to put this machine in my office and every week before I place my order you want me to look up the titles you have in stock and write down the title codes of the titles I need. Then you want me to call your operators and place my order using these numbers. On top of all of this, you want me to pay quarterly fees for the system, so that I as a customer can order from you. You're crazy! I would never pay a vendor so that I could order from him."

The buyer saw the crestfallen look on my face and, being a nice person, said, "It's break time. Let me buy you a cup of coffee in the cafeteria."

While walking from the office to the coffee shop, the buyer was very quiet. I was hoping she was thinking over the benefits of a weekly microfiche program.

A few minutes later, sitting over a cup of coffee, the buyer interrupted my comments on the weather. "Wait a minute. I think I see how it can work," she said. She thought a few moments longer. "It is convenient, up-to-date, fast. . . . We will have all the information we need to make good buying decisions. . . ." Finally she said, "Really, this just might be the greatest system I have ever seen. I will pay you whatever you ask to get it."

Of course I was ecstatic. The program had won. I returned to my company, developed a strong presentation for book retailers, and within eighteen months ten thousand retailers throughout the country had subscribed to the program.

I did not employ a brilliant strategy to achieve this goal. Instead, I "put myself in the customer's shoes"—in this case, the shoes of the retail bookseller. Being aware of the retailer's needs was my top priority.

I did make a point of broadening my knowledge whenever the opportunity presented itself, even if it was not immediately apparent how the information could be of help. I also used contact with a personal friend, and I employed persistence in getting the program developed.

But the most important thing was to put myself in the shoes of the customer. This approach led to the development of a program that was later copied by every book wholesaler in the country.

Today the wholesaler that started the system is the largest book wholesaler in the world, and microfiche, even in this day of sophisticated computer networks, is being used by thousands of bookstores in the United States.

Vision

Leaders in business experience their greatest failures when they lack the vision necessary to keep an enterprise growing in difficult times.

Most aspiring people would like to have this said about them: "This is a person with vision." This descriptive phrase connotes a person who sees the future clearly and who marches toward that future with assurance and certainty—a person who can be among the trees and still see the forest.

Those who have vision are few. Like good instincts, vision seems to be something a person is born with and yet, also like good instincts, vision can be developed.

Leaders often forget the banality of an ordinary life. Not only can power corrupt, it often disengages the powerful from everyday life's reality. Because they don't understand how things work for the average person, they lose the ability to direct their enterprise. A leader who does not empathize with the needs of the people who perform the job or with the customer who buys the product will not be able to make the visionary changes necessary to keep the enterprise going when times get rough.

Your vision must include a commitment to continually add value to the product you are selling. Your product or service must never rest on its laurels. There must always be something in development that will lead to improvement. This is the responsibility of all the leaders within the enterprise, not just the CEO. You must be constantly thinking of ways to improve your company's products and services. Even if you don't have the authority to make the actual changes, you must develop a way of looking at the product or service as you would if you were the end user. This will help you come up with ideas for improvements.

As you develop your vision, try to be completely aware of what your competitor is doing. It is especially important to be aware of any action by competing companies that might affect your business. If you are going to use fear at all, make it your rule to remain in constant fear that your competitor will do something better than you do. You will find yourself continually developing new products or services. The Japanese have a word for this, *kaizen*, which means a constant state of trying to improve.

Being First

Those who copy are usually unable to build a better program or even come close to the success of the originators.

Being first with a good idea means that others who copy the idea may never catch up, especially if they are late in copying—unless you become lazy and let them "add on" to the idea more quickly and in better ways than your own company does. If you are first with a good idea in your business, and you continue to improve it constantly, you will watch your company attain leadership in the marketplace.

When I first went to Waldenbooks, one of the things I noticed about our competition as well as ourselves was that none of us sold magazines. I immediately had a program developed to retrofit all our stores with sizable magazine racks. It was extremely important for us to be the first to carry a large selection of magazines. Putting magazines in the bookstores was one of the reasons Waldenbooks went from a poor second to become the dominant bookseller in America in the '80s and the very early '90s.

When Leadership Fails

Successful leaders put the welfare
of their people above all else.

T here is no question that the biggest crisis America
faces today is a lack of leadership. From the presidency
to Congress to the business community, our leaders
have failed. They have failed because they do not have the
vision necessary to develop workable solutions to the
problems their consitituents face. They have failed because
they have not responded to the needs of the people.

In politics, the power of big special-interest groups has
prevented lawmakers from taking bipartisan action to do
what must be done to provide an environment that will
enable people to help themselves. Many lawmakers have
allowed their egos, their greed, and the fear of losing
their jobs to control their actions, and thus have failed to
do the right thing for the people. It seems that many
politicians of today have lost sight of their primary
responsibility—that of doing what is right for America.

In business it is much the same. Business leaders have
not responded to the needs of the people who work the
enterprise, or to the needs of the customers who buy the
products of that enterprise. Instead they have succumbed
to the pressures of Wall Street. The analysts who look for

short-term results have become so obsessed with the power their positions give them that they will do whatever is necessary to preserve that power, often at the expense of their employees, their customers, and the enterprise itself. It is sad that when a major company announces a major cutback in jobs, the stock market usually responds favorably by pushing up the price of the stock, ignoring the fact that the company has failed its people and brought misery to thousands of families.

I am not denying that in business and politics hard decisions that will have a negative effect on people must sometimes be made. A sudden downturn in the economy may necessitate unfortunate layoffs. In politics especially, no decision will be liked by every single constituent. But if the policies of government and business were developed with the best interests of the people in mind, hardships would be minimal.

Us against Them

Think of the competition as the enemy.

In 1997, a major U.S. manufacturer announced that its profits would not meet analysts' expectations. The company's stock price dropped precipitously, and the CEO advised that he would make an announcement in the near future. When he finally took the podium a few weeks later, he started with a weak bit of humor and then proceeded to announce that the company was laying off ten thousand employees. During the course of his announcement he extolled the virtues of his management team and said that "much had been accomplished in the past three years." These accomplishments were obviously not enough to prevent ten thousand people from losing their jobs, which affected another forty thousand people (the families of those who were laid off), not to mention their communities.

In anticipation of the announcement, the company's stock had begun to climb. Although some Wall Street analysts didn't think he had gone far enough, the CEO received the plaudits of the pundits, and stockholders were probably happy. No one seemed to blame the CEO or his management team for the poor profit results or for disrupting the lives of thousands. The CEO and probably all of his valued management team got to keep their jobs.

While at times serious national economic problems unfortunately make layoffs a necessity, companies usually run into problems of this type because the senior managers of the company have become complacent and tolerant of competitors. They believe their company is invincible to attack or injury. In this manufacturer's case, lack of vision and creativity as well as tolerance of the competition were reasons for the company's inability to keep a competitor from taking a significant share of the market.

It seems virtually impossible that a company that at one time completely dominated a field could allow a company with very little share of the market to take significant amounts of its business. And yet it happened. Unless the senior team shows some vision and creativity, and takes positive action against the competition, their market share will continue to erode.

I have always believed that unless the competition is considered to be the "hated enemy" by everyone in the organization, and unless everyone in the organization does everything legally possible to beat the "enemy," chances are good that a competitor or competitors will in some way harm the business. The CEO should be able to make this the mission of the organization, but even if he or she doesn't, anyone in the lower echelons who takes on this mission can have a positive effect on the business.

Most of the things that I did as a manager and later as a CEO were done because beating the competition was my highest priority. I would scout the competition with intensity and, if I saw an opportunity to do something different or better, I would pursue the effort with even greater intensity. Why was this my mission? Because my true mission was to do everything I could to protect the interests of the people in our organization.

The "hated enemy" theory may not play as well today as it did a few years ago. Some may prefer to talk about "us against them." But the valuable part of this way of thinking remains the same. Animosity should not be directed toward your own people, but toward the people who are doing everything in their power to drive your organization into the ground.

Did I really think of our competitors as the "hated enemy"? I recall seeing the heads of rival companies socializing, acting as friends. I never understood how they could do that. Those were the people who were threats to the livelihood of everyone in my organization as well as myself, and I did not consider them friends.

A former associate smilingly reminded me of what I told him twenty-five years ago, after he joined my company as a young man in his early twenties. "You told me there are two kinds of people in the world: they are either the customer or the enemy."

Mission Statements

Don't waste time on words that do not address the real interests of the people working the enterprise.

I have always disliked mission statements. Often a mission statement is a collection of beautiful words that proclaim goals that may have little relation to the real interests of the people working the enterprise. A mission statement may be a lengthy document imposed on people by management—in which case the people are usually not inspired. If you are going to create a mission statement for your company, be sure that all who will implement the mission have a part in creating it, if only to give their opinions.

For me, the most important mission of all people who work an enterprise is to keep the business healthy, to protect the jobs of the people working the enterprise, and to make it possible for all in the company to achieve a better life.

The best way to do this is by constantly beating the competition and fixing things that ain't broke.

Being Competitive

Make good use of your natural competitiveness.

Competitiveness is a natural human trait, and it is especially strong in some individuals. Some believe that being competitive is an undesirable quality, which should be stamped out. I believe that, like all human traits, it can be used in positive or negative ways. Competition within an organization can be productive, as people vie to come up with better ideas or do better work than their colleagues.

Competition outside the organization is less friendly, though no less useful. If you are too friendly with your competitors, it can undermine your drive to protect the interests of your own organization.

Am I naturally competitive? My children recall watching me at the helm of my sailboat, doing everything in my power to pull ahead of another sailboat that was sailing a little to starboard. When I finally pulled ahead, leaving the other boat in my wake, I said with satisfaction: "We beat them!"

"Dad!" my daughter said with chagrin. "*They* weren't even *racing!*"

If You Want to Become a CEO

Ten things you should do.

Becoming a CEO requires many different skills and a lot of luck. Skills are gained primarily through very hard work and exposing yourself to a lot of information. While being in the right place at the right time is often pure luck, a complete understanding of a company and its personnel can go a long way in helping to position yourself. The ten things on this list can be very helpful in achieving your goals.

1. Work harder than everyone else!
2. Remember that appearance can make a difference.
3. Become the ultimate consumer.
4. Know your competition better than anyone.
5. Know (in great detail) the financial condition of your company.
6. Do things willingly.
7. Love the business you are in.
8. Always protect the people you manage.
9. Always try to improve your company.
10. Work harder than anyone else . . .

1. Work harder than everyone else!

Working harder than everyone else usually means you are the first to begin work in the morning and the last to leave at night. It means at least ten hours a day, five days a week, and usually a half day on Saturday. It means working at home at night to prepare for the next day. It means that you will have less time for your family and leisure pursuits. If you run out of things to do in your regular job, find other things to do that will increase your knowledge of the company. If your company is in the distribution business, spend time working in the warehouse. If your company has a sales organization and you are not a salesperson, work with someone who is. If your company has retail stores, work in the stores. You must also be willing to relocate at the company's request. In most cases, a move is a promotion. Be aware, however, that if your new location is away from the home office, you will have to work even harder to establish your reputation with those who run things at the home office.

2. Remember that appearance can make a difference.

Always look your best. If you are out of shape, get in shape and stay that way. Always dress as well as your budget can afford. Avoid being ostentatious. Try to have an upbeat demeanor: it is contagious, and people will respond favorably to you and your positive attitude.

3. Become the ultimate consumer.

Be a customer of the products or services your company offers so that you will understand their strengths and weaknesses. Once you know how to do this you will be able to offer suggestions on how to make things better. This will also allow you to be creative in developing new products and services that fit into the company's capacity.

4. Know your competition better than anyone.

Knowing your competition means trying to understand their business as well as your own. What are their strengths and weaknesses? What is their corporate culture? Do they have an outstanding CEO or one who is mediocre? How creative and visionary are they? What do they do better than your company? Where do they fail to measure up? What is their financial situation? How are their sales? Once you know all that is possible to know, you will be able to evaluate and develop the things your company can do, in both the short run and the long run, to be better than your competitors.

5. Know (in great detail) the financial condition of your company.

Regardless of what department you are in, study the financial condition of your company. Know where the company is strong and where weakness exists. Be able to interpret all aspects of the financial statements. Knowing the financial condition of the company in great detail will in most cases put you far ahead of your peers, and will help immensely as your career progresses.

6. Do things willingly.

Often when assignments are handed out, the "assignee" may have negative thoughts about his or her particular assignment. While these negative thoughts may not be outwardly expressed, the person handing out the assignment will feel the negativism. Even though you may not like an assignment, you must accept it willingly and do your best to complete it in the best way possible. If the assignment is flawed, you will be in a better position to expose its flaws if you have shown willingness to undertake the assignment in the first place.

7. Love the business you are in.

It will help a lot of you really love the business you have chosen. My first job was selling soap to grocery stores in the Upper East Side of New York City. I hated it. At first I worked harder than anyone else, but I soon found that my dislike for the business tempered my ardor for advancement. I found myself not working as hard as I should to achieve my goals. While I was fortunate enough to receive a couple of promotions and eventually managed seven or eight salespeople, I never liked the job. Later, when I had the good fortune to secure a job in the book business, I found that I really loved this business. My association with book publishers, book retailers, and book wholesalers was always enjoyable. My love for the business helped immeasurably in advancing my career.

8. Always protect the people you manage.

Smiling and showing recognition are two ways you can show people that you care about them. Using creativity, vision, and hard work to keep your organization healthy and strong is a fundamental way of showing caring and protecting jobs. Protecting your people also means that you take responsibility for what they do. This responsibility includes the work they do as well as their health and welfare while performing that work.

9. Always try to improve your company.

From company policy to product or service presentation to the product or service itself, you must always be thinking of how things can be made better for the customer. Think creatively about any product or service your company offers, letting your mind freewheel as you write down the thoughts that come to you. You will be surprised at the results.

10. Work harder than anyone else. . . .

The final thing you must do to become a CEO is the same as the first because it is the most important. You will probably have to sacrifice a lot during the early stages of your career, but if you are successful, you will feel a great deal of satisfaction. When the time comes to retire, you will be able to say that you accomplished your goal.